EPITAPHS
AND IMAGES
FROM SCOTTISH
GRAVEYARDS

EPITAPHS
AND IMAGES
FROM SCOTTISH
GRAVEYARDS

BETTY WILLSHER

CANONGATE

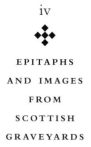

iv

**EPITAPHS
AND IMAGES
FROM
SCOTTISH
GRAVEYARDS**

To Penny

Photographs by Betty Willsher, copyright RCAHMS.

ACKNOWLEDGMENTS

The author wishes to thank Nigel Tranter for permission to quote from 'Luss Village', the Society of Antiquaries of Scotland for assistance in recording old gravestones in all of the Lowland parishes, and RCAHMS for permission to use the photographs taken by me for the National Monument Records. I am grateful to my friends the late Doreen Mould, Jess Nelson and Neil Foston, for their help and encouragement.

HALF TITLE PAGE.
Here lies the body of 'The Gentleman Beggar', Andrew Gemmels alias Edie Ochiltree the prototype of Scott's character in *The Antiquary*. He died at Roxburgh Newtown in 1793 aged 106 years. Stone erected 1849.

TITLE PAGE.
Detail. Greyfriars Burial Ground, Perth. John Young, candle maker, 1745.

First published in 1996 in the UK by
Canongate Books Ltd
14 High Street, Edinburgh EH1 1TE

Text © Betty Willsher 1996
Photographs by Betty Willsher, © RCAHMS

The moral rights of the author have been asserted

Extract from 'Luss Village' from *Collected Poems* by Iain Crichton Smith
is reproduced by kind permission of Carcanet Press Ltd

Cataloguing-In-Publication-Data
A catalogue record for this title is available
upon request from the British Library

ISBN 0 86241 591 8

Book design by Mark Blackadder

Printed and bound in the UK by Butler & Tanner, Frome, Somerset

CONTENTS

❖

DETAIL.
TILLICOULTRY
CHURCHYARD,
CLACKMANNANSHIRE,
N.D.

1

INTRODUCTION
THE STONES CRY OUT

IN THE CHURCHYARD
THE TILTED TOMBS STILL GOSSIP, AND THE LEAVES
OF STONY TESTAMENTS ARE READ BY RICHARD,
JEAN AND CAROL, PERT AMONG THE SHEAVES
OF UNSCYTHED SHADOWS, WHILE THE NOON DAY HUMS
WITH BEES AND WATER AND THE GHOST OF PSALMS.

From 'Luss Village' by Iain Crichton Smith

The most satisfying way to read an epitaph is to decipher it from a gravestone in the kirkyard. The stone is a marker to identify the exact spot where someone, familiar or strange, was buried; the epitaph is the key to his or her identity. It may be as long ago as three centuries that an anonymous mason using chisel and hammer patiently inscribed, word by word, the chosen message. According to the region, the era, and personal choice you may first read 'HIC IACET' or many variations such as 'HERE LAYETH THE BODY/THE CORPSE/THE DUST/THE DUST AND ASHES/THE REMAINS'; or, 'HERE LYES IN HOPE OF A GLORIOUS RESURRECTION', or simply 'In memory of'. Or if it is a man, it may begin 'HERE LYES ANE HONEST MAN' or 'HERE LYES ANE HONORABLE MAN'. Then — with luck — his name is revealed, the place where he lived, his occupation, the date of his death, and his age. You may also discover the relationship with the person who erected the monument, and other members of the family who were later buried there.

There may be a rhyming epitaph on the memorial you are studying. If the lettering is obscured by lichen or if the stone is flaking or sunk in the earth, with mounting curiosity and determination you meet the challenge; with gently searching fingers, word by word you decipher the lines. What will this poem reveal? Most likely it is a message expanding the omnipresent succinct warning 'Memento Mori' (Remember Death), but most epitaphs give the message of hope, the promise of eternal life.

Of special interest — if this is a memorial to one of your ancestors — you may find a eulogy on his virtues, or a description of the trade or profession he followed, or of the way in which he died. You may also learn about the feelings and the philosophy of those who mourned his loss.

The following inscription on a headstone at Panbride, Angus, reminds us of the antiquity of the custom of setting up memorials to individuals.

In memory of Jacob's love
Unto his Rachel now above,
A pillar of stone we read he gave,
And sett it up upon her grave;
The first and ancient to be seen
In Genesis the 35 & 19.

ELIZABETH SMITH, PANBRIDE, 1759

This was erected by a merchant in memory of his wife. The practice of commemorating the dead by composing epitaphs in prose and poetry was an ancient one. Sometimes the epitaph was inscribed on the tomb, in which case it might take the form of a notice giving the name and age and station of the deceased, as was so often the case on Roman tombs. In addition, or

PREVIOUS PAGE.
DETAIL.
ROBERT BROWN
AND MARY SYM,
KILMALIEU, INVERARY,
ARGYLLSHIRE.
+1699

OPPOSITE.
PART OF THE
KIRKYARD AT
ST PETERS, DUFFUS,
MORAY

4

❖❖❖

EPITAPHS
AND IMAGES
FROM
SCOTTISH
GRAVEYARDS

occasionally alternatively, there might be a poem or a prose epitaph in praise of the dead person, or one of mourning, or of philosophising, as in the case of Greek inscriptions. In *Chronicles of the Tombs*, Pettigrew gives examples of epitaphs from the Greeks, the Romans, and Saxons. The lines from Horace's *Odes* must be familiar to many:

> Pallida Mors aequo pulsat pede pauperum
> tabernas Regumque turris.
> *Pale death with impartial foot knocks on the doors*
> *of poor men's hovels and of king's palaces.*

As will be seen later, this is one of many ancient themes which fascinated mourners down the centuries, themes which were adopted and put into different forms, according to place and time. Renaissance writers were greatly influenced by *The Greek Anthology*, and from short sweet poems of praise in that ancient collection came phrases such as 'Here lies', 'Tread softly', and 'Stop traveller'. Another major influence was the Roman writer Martial, the composer of epigrams and epitaphs which were witty, harsh, and sometimes indecent. In Britain, from the sixteenth century onwards the poets of the day delighted in composing verses of both sorts.

Soon after the Reformation in Scotland an edict was issued that there should be no further burials within churches. As some city churchyards were already filled with bodies laid to rest in unmarked graves, provision was made in Edinburgh, Perth and Dundee to use the grounds of the abandoned Greyfriars monasteries. In other cities and towns, Cathedral and Abbey precincts were made available when there was a need. Handsome carved tombs soon lined the walls of Greyfriars Burial Ground in Edinburgh; in spite of Death being deemed a leveller, mural monuments and outside aisles had prestige, and the size and grandeur of the monument were reflections of wealth and status. On such grand seventeenth-century tombs, at least part of the epitaph, if not all, was in Latin. At St Andrews Cathedral Burial Ground a group of richly adorned tablestones — many to merchants and tradesmen or their spouses — were erected to the north-west of the Cathedral; (these are now in the Cathedral Visitors' Centre). Similarly at the Howff, Dundee, at Greyfriars, Perth, and elsewhere, monuments inscribed with epitaphs flourished in a gradually increasing democracy of death.

The earliest collection of English epitaphs was compiled by John Weever in 1631. In the preface he expresses annoyance at what he considers to be an improper use of both monuments and epitaphs. Both had been the prerogative of 'Royalty and the Nobility, the Eminent and such as were of Vertu, Wisdom and Valour'. But now the practice was being abused in commemorating 'rich quondam Tradesmen and griping useres'.

In 1704 another volume of epitaphs was published. This book by Robert Monteith bore the imposing title *Ane Theater of Mortality or the Illustrious Inscriptions extant upon several Monuments erected over the Dead-Bodies (of the sometime Honourable Persons) Buried within the Greyfriars Church-yard; and other Churches and Burial Places within the City of Edinburgh and Suburbs Collected and Englished by R. Monteith.* The philosophy and the sentiments expressed on these grand tombs no doubt served as models for those who, throughout the eighteenth century, composed epitaphs to suit individual circumstances.

However, this book became rare, and in 1834 there appeared *Collection of Epitaphs and Monumental Inscriptions in Scotland.* It contained the entire Monteith collection. In addition, Mr William Dobie of Beith and 'several literary gentlemen' furnished the publisher, Mr Macvean of Glasgow, with similar epitaphs from the university cities and from town and country parishes. The usefulness of this book is that it included some of the humble and often quaint epitaphs written by local people.

In 1857 Thomas Joseph Pettigrew published *Chronicles of the Tombs, A Select Collection of Epitaphs preceded by An Essay of Epitaphs and other monumental inscription.* Most usefully, Pettigrew classifies the epitaphs. The headings are interesting — I have changed the order to indicate which were the most popular in seventeenth and eighteenth-century Scotland; first: Admonitory, Devotional and Scriptural; second: Laudatory and Adulatory; third: Historical and Professional; fourth: Condemnatory, Deprecatory and Denunciatory; fifth: Punning, Acrostic, Enigmatical, and Chronogrammatic; sixth: Satirical and Ridiculous. With regard to the satirical and ridiculous, in Scotland such verses may have been written and may have been published; they may have been passed on in oral tradition; but they were very seldom carved on gravestones. The reasons are discussed in the last section of this book.

The widespread interest in the subject of epitaphs continued. During the late nineteenth century Dr Charles Rogers' two volumes of *Scottish Monuments and Tombstones* appeared in 1871. He presents the epitaphs according to geographical location, that is arranged by the old counties. His book gives a wider selection, but many are undated and unnamed. Not so those in the two volumes by Andrew Jervise, *Epitaphs and Monumental Inscriptions in North-East Scotland.* The recordings which Jervise made were meticulous, and of great value to the genealogist and local historian. He worked in an area where epitaphs abound. It should be remembered that the majority of people were buried without a monument to mark their graves; but in fertile regions where there was a degree of prosperity, such as Angus and East and Mid Lothians, masons received many commissions. Some of the stones which Monteith and Jervise recorded have disappeared. It is very regrettable that kirkyard monuments have been lost over the centuries. For instance, the early slabs at Greyfriars, Perth, were removed by Cromwell to use in building a fort. In the nineteenth century in the town graveyards stones were removed because, until cemeteries were provided, there was a demand for space. Also some town graveyards were 'tidied up' — loss from this cause still continues.

In the late 1950s Sheila and John Fowler Mitchell, on behalf of the Scottish Genealogy Society, began the immense task of recording monumental inscriptions on Scottish gravestones, county by county. Assisted by the family and a few volunteers, their achievements up to the time of their retirement were immense. Individuals and local groups have carried on the work and it is now nearing completion. Alison Mitchell's editorial references are most useful. Some copies are available from the Scottish Genealogy Society, and local libraries stock the relevant volumes.

Apart from Pettigrew, none of the authors of the above collections showed an interest in the style of the epitaph. Pettigrew recommends 'the expression of thoughts in the clearest and easiest way, with the best chosen words for hearing and sound'. He condemned the strongly expressive, those which were stiff and those which were affected. It was generally agreed that the epitaph should be brief in expression. Pettigrew quotes Richard Puttenham in *The Arte of English Poesie* (1659) as stating that epitaphs should be 'pithie, quick & sententious'. This is not always the case, though the space available fortunately sets limits. Some of the best known epitaphs (not necessarily appearing on the monuments) were written by Shakespeare, Ben Johnson, Spencer, Goldsmith, and Pope; and in Scotland by Robert Burns and later Sir Walter Scott. Pope's verses were the epitome of wit and brevity, but not always acceptable even to the more liberal English Church. For example:

Nature and Nature's Laws hid Night
God said LET NEWTON BE and all was bright.

John Gay wrote for his own tomb:

Life is a jest & all things show it
I thought so once and now I know it.

There is something to be said for epitaphs which waste no words. The following are by unknown Scottish authors: the first from the gravestone of James Low who died in 1752 at Strathmartine, Angus.

Thy name aye, thy fame aye,
Shall never be cutt off;
Thy grave ay, shall have ay,
Thy honest epitaph.

Equally simple are the lines on a tombstone at Dundonald, Ayr, on the 1761 headstone of Janet MacFadzon, the wife of a pedlar.

> It will not be by tuck of drum,
> But it will be with trumpet's sound,
> And then I'll my Redeemer see,
> Who shed his precious blood for me.

Many of the recurrent themes used on seventeenth and eighteenth-century Scottish monuments have come from earlier tombs. On Shakespeare's tombstone in Holy Trinity Church in Stratford-upon-Avon is inscribed

> GOOD FREND FOR IESVS SAKE FORBEARE,
> TO DIGG THE DVST ENCLOASED HERE:
> BLESTE BE YE MAN YT SPARES THES STONES
> AND CVRST BE HE YT MOVES MY BONES.

At Maryton, Angus, a blacksmith, whose name is lost, an epitaph from the distant past warns us in quaint terms:

> WO. bE. TO
> HIM. yAT. PU
> TIS. yIS, TOO
> ANy. WDER.
> W S . W H A
> dESECIT.IN.A
> NOA. MXCLX
> XX1V. yN.yAR

> (Woe be to him whom puts this [gravestone] to
> any other use, who died in anno 1660 24 in year).

At Jedburgh two centuries later Baillie Thomas Winter had inscribed on his tombstone, 'Whoever removes this stone or causes it to be removed, may he die the last of his race'. Shakespeare's concept of 'All the world's a stage' re-appears in the line found quite frequently, for example on the monument at Inverarity, Angus, to Thomas Mill who died in 1765:

> Here lyes a sober honest man,
> As any in an age,
> But by and by Death struck him down,
> And turned him off the stage.

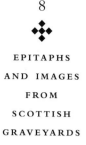
A small group of epitaphs appears all over Britain and some were used on gravestones in New England. There are many variations of the sailor's one, the following at Forgan, Fife is to Androw Adam, who died in 1758 aged 11 years:

Tho Boreas and Nepto his waves
Hath toss'd me to and fro,
Yet by the order of God's decree,
I harrbour here below,
Where now I lie at anchor sure,
With many of owre fleet,
Expecting on[e] day to sail
My Admiral to meet.

This may originate from Francis Quarles' *Emblems Divine and Moral* (1635):

Let Boreas blasts & Neptune's waves be join'd,
Thy Aeolus commands the waves, the winds
Fear not the rocks, a world imperious crew,
That climbs't a Rock, my soul! a rock?

Another popular and varied theme is:

Afflictions sore with meekness long I bore,
Physicians were in vain;
Till God did please that death should seize
And eas'd me of my pain.
(THIS FROM KILBIRNIE, AGNES ALLAN, 1775)

The following lines are familiar:

No costly marble
Need on her be spent;
Her deathless worth
Is her best monument.
(FROM PEEBLES, ANNE HAY, 1804)

Children are often likened to flowers. At Glamis, Angus, on the tombstone of James Rhynd who died in 1734, aged 1 year 5 months, are the lines:

Here lies a sweet and loving child,
Ah, cover'd o'er with mud,
Resembling well the lillie fair,
Cropt in the very bud.

The stone books in the kirkyards offered wonderful opportunities for proclaiming the teachings of the Reformed Church. For the sources of many one must turn to the Bible, both the Old and New Testaments, and to the metrical psalms. Indeed the greatest influence on these Scottish epitaphs was the religious teaching of the time. This source is more evident in Scotland than in England.

Are such epitaphs to be found in every Scottish graveyard? In the Highlands and in some regions of the Scottish Lowlands most of the seventeenth and eighteenth-century stones are comparatively plain, with a minimum of information and few carved emblems. The elaborately carved stones are found in those areas where there was a supply of freestone, which allowed the masons to decorate the stone with emblems, biblical scenes, portraits of the deceased, shields or cartouches, flowers, designs and epitaphs. Usually the cutters of these stones were local parish masons whose identity has not yet been discovered. They tried, through a mason-customer agreement, to make a unique stone for each customer.

The emblems of mortality and immortality came from a common repertoire, established in Protestant countries after the Reformation. The masons — and sometimes their customers — selected from the range, using myriad permutations. These carvings presented in pictorial form a message which might be echoed in the epitaph, in prose or in rhyming verse. It is these rhyming epitaphs, mainly of the seventeenth and eighteenth centuries, which we will consider. They are, in a way, similar to the emblems: variations on a body of universally established themes. The ideas for the epitaphs come from the scriptures, the popular emblem books and the work of writers, scholars and poets. The masons may have had a stock of epitaphs from which the customer could choose, amending them to suit the customers' taste. But it is evident that established poets, local ministers, school teachers, and rhymsters were requested to make new versions for individual needs.

Throughout the eighteenth century the headstone was the monument of the people. Ordinary folk saved up their money, and were proud that they could commemorate their loved ones and proclaim their philosophy of death. A Scottish feature was that the masons tended to use both sides of the headstone so that there was space for a profusion of carvings, and both notices and poems. In spite of the Calvinistic abhorrence of imagery, the graveyard monuments were carved with meaningful emblems and biblical scenes. Death called for an expression of feeling. Many memorials have rhyming epitaphs which echo the message given by the emblems of mortality and immortality. In the case of others the verse has little connection with the carving. Sometimes the masons and their customers chose to fill the space with carvings (such as a full portrait taking up a face of a headstone); others concentrated on minimal carvings and a detailed notice and poem. There are

but a few unique stones where picture and epitaph make an integrated composition. Consequently the epitaphs which follow are divided into themes, and the photographs are from a selection of stones which have carvings related to the theme. Many of the epitaphs and images are from Angus graveyards, where there was a supply of sandstone easy to carve and comparatively durable, and communities able to afford such monuments.

On reading the collections from the grand tombs — whether in prose or poetry — given by Monteith and by Pettigrew, one is likely to become satiated with the adulation and the declamation. It may be wise to 'dip into' a book of epitaphs rather than read one after the other. Each was intended for a unique occasion, and has with it special feelings. They contrast with epitaphs to the humble Scots; there is a quality of freshness, an endearing quaintness in the naivety and in the spelling; the homespun quality is appealing. A mixture of words in Latin, English, and the Scots tongue make curious reading. Quotations from the Bible, and Hebrew and Greek and Gaelic phrases may be found. With the coming of the eighteenth century, the notices and epitaphs, in verse or prose, were increasingly written in polite fashionable English.

Upper case lettering was replaced by many variations: a mixture of upper and lower case, sloped and looped writing, copybook characters, and eventually Gothic script. In the poems occasional words reveal the spoken dialect. The rhyming word may not always seem a match, but if you recall how it was spoken, it fits. In some epitaphs the iambic pentameter is achieved and is successful; other models are imperfectly followed and the scansion has the flaws and the charm of the folk art carvings.

Sometimes the date of the erection of a monument is inscribed; sometimes it may be assessed from the entry, or entries, of the date(s) of the death of the deceased. There may be later entries, indicated by a change in the style of lettering. Some stones were revised, and a further date added. In this book the date of death of the deceased (one or more than one) is given. If the date is indecipherable the letters n.d. (for no date) are used. Captions are placed below the given epitaph when it illustrates a point or a theme, but are placed above the epitaph when it describes a person or persons, as, for example, in eulogies.

The study of epitaphs is not morbid because the messages are usually of hope. They may bring moments of sadness, of a softening sympathy over the losses of so many infants, children and people in their prime, and feelings that in some ways we live in more fortunate times. But you read of good deeds, of kind people, of strange events, of comfort and cheerful optimism, of respect, admiration and love. How strange, these words carved in stone from long-forgotten people, who, as we think of them, live again.

PENNINGHAME OLD
CHURCHYARD,
WIGTOWNSHIRE,
JAMES HERON 1738.
A WONDERFUL
EXAMPLE
OF A MASON'S
SKILL AND
ORIGINALITY

BATHGATE,
WEST LOTHIAN,
THOMAS JERVIE,
1705. AN EARLY
EIGHTEENTH-CENTURY
EXAMPLE OF UPPER
AND LOWER CASE
LETTERING. THIS
PARTICULAR STONE
SHOWS A PLEASING
INDIVIDUALITY.
ABOVE THE
INSCRIPTION IS A
SERENE WINGED
SOUL TUCKED
UNDER A FOLIATE
HEAD, THE GREEN
MASK REVEALING
THE HUMAN MOUTH
AND CHIN.
DETAIL OPPOSITE.

2

PULVIS ET UMBRA SUMUS

WE ARE BUT DUST AND

SHADOWS

❖❖❖

PULVIS
ET UMBRA
SUMUS
WE ARE
BUT DUST
AND
SHADOWS

In times past, Death, ever-present, ever-dreaded, swooped on the young and innocent: on the bread-winners, young wives and mothers and those in their prime. The ubiquitous symbols carved on the tombs and referred to in epitaphs were the skull and the bones, gruesome images from the charnel house. But there were many others — the skeleton of the deceased, the hourglass, the tools of the sexton (spade and turf cutter), Death's dart and Father Time's scythe, the deid bell, the coffin, the serpent. Death was personified as the King of Terrors and carved on the gravestones as a skeleton with dart in hand, or weilding scythe, predatory or in the act of killing. Father Time, his accomplice, appears with scythe and hourglass (opposite). The masons drew on scenes from the religious, didactic Emblem Books of Francis Quarles, so popular in the seventeenth and eighteenth centuries, and occasionally an entire illustration was cut on a tombstone with the appropriate text. An example is the Judith Nairn stone at St Andrews Cathedral, Fife.

The next page shows shows a panel from this ornate coped stone which has four scenes, this one from Book V Epigram XII. A woman stands in front of a curtain, and a robed figure representing Christ appears outside at the end of the curtain. The text is from Psalm xlii, verse 2, 'When shall I come and appear before God?' Each illustration and text in 'Emblems' is accompanied by devoutly religious poetry by Quarles.

The presentation of emblems of mortality may seem morbid, but was balanced by the other side of the Church's message; that death is inevitable but only the sinful body dies. The immortal part, man's soul, soars upwards to the heavens, there awaiting the Day of Judgement. The Reformation brought hope to every man and woman alike, whatever their social standing; all were capable of seeking grace.

Another form of symbolism, the dual emblem, became popular in the eighteenth century. The doused downward torch of death was balanced by the flaming torch of immortality. Palm fronds, rings of greenery, cornucopia with fruit, leaf fronds and roses all signified the hope of Paradise, the renewal of life. Accordingly a skull sprouting leaves, serpents spewing out fronds, gave the two-fold message of 'I die to live'. Most curious of all, and an almost exclusively Scottish feature on post-Reformation tombs, is the foliate head. There are 160 recorded tombstones dating between 1667 and 1800 which bear this emblem. This grotesque head with greenery sprouting from it originated in Rome in the last part of the first century AD. When crops were threatened, Dionysiac rites were carried out, originally with human or animal sacrifices. The ceremonies became symbolic, and those partaking covered their faces with leaves. The motif of the leaf mask was translated into Christian iconography by a strange chance. In the sixth century AD a cathedral was being built in the Roman-occupied town of Trier. Foliate masks from a Roman temple which had occupied the site were put into the new fabric. These served as a model for later masons and became very popular; they went through various changes in

❖❖❖

OPPOSITE.
CORSTORPHINE,
EDINBURGH,
FRANCIS GLOAG,
1736.
FATHER TIME
WITH SCYTHE AND
HOURGLASS IS
FLANKED BY
FLAMING URNS.

character and in meaning. In church architecture and on medieval tombs the greenery is often spewed from the mouth of a hideous face which has a malevolent leer, or a scowling glare, fangs or ugly teeth. It may be in human or in animal form. It was said to represent the sins of wicked and lustful men. Examples are to be found in the ruins or museums of Scottish abbeys, such as Glen Luce, Melrose and Jedburgh; of cathedrals — Elgin, Dunkeld, St Andrews, Glasgow — and in the fabric of medieval churches — St Bryde's, Douglas, Leuchars, Dalmeny. Recently the foliate heads have acquired the name 'Green Men', but should not be confused with other figures which come from various sources and have various significances.

There are many types of foliate heads on our tombstones; that this ugly pagan emblem was condoned by our Calvinist churchmen seems extraordinary. The only epitaph which is linked to this emblem was a popular one, 'though after my skin worms devour my body, yet in my flesh shall I see God'. On the Milne monument in Greyfriars Churchyard in Edinburgh, there are four examples, two of which are shown on the opposite page.

These seem to be the earliest green men. This notable family of architects, master masons to the Stuart kings, would be well acquainted with the foliate head. At Rosslyn Chapel there is a fantastic array. This was a vivid addition to the range of emblems; a dual symbolism in that the ugly head represented the death of the sinful body and the greenery the Resurrection.

THE TYRANT DEATH

IN TYME DISPONE, DEATH COMES ANON
AND NOTHING WITH HIM GETS,
BVT EVN SHORT SHEET, OUER HEAD AND FEET,
AND ALL MEN HIM FORGETS.

KETTINS, ANGUS, ELSPETH JACK, 1684

OF TERROUR'S KING THE TROPHIES HERE YOU SEE;
FRAIL MAN! HIS DAYS LIKE TO A SHADOW FLEE,
OR LIKE THE PATH OF EAGLE'S WINGS ON HIGH,
THAT LEAVES NO TRACES ON THE DISTANT SKY;
FAIR AS THESE FLOWERS THAT FLEETING FADE AWAY
SO DOES LIFE EXPAND, THEN DROOP, DECAY!
BUT FUTURE SPRINGS SHALL RENOVATE THE TOMB,
AND WE, IN GARDENS OF TH'ETERNAL, BLOOM.

KINGHORN, FIFE, WILLIAM KNOX, 1677

**PULVIS
ET UMBRA
SUMUS**
*WE ARE
BUT DUST
AND
SHADOWS*

TOP.
ST ANDREWS
CATHEDRAL MUSEUM,
FIFE. DETAIL
JUDITH NAIRN,
1646

BOTTOM.
GREYFRIARS BURIAL
GROUND, EDINBURGH,
JOHN MILNE, 1667.
THE DETAIL SHOWS
TWO OF THE FOUR
UGLY FOLIATE
HEADS.

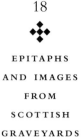
Oh, death how fierce thy firy Blows,
No forrester like thee;
Cuts down the cedar while it grows
And spares the weathered tree.

MEIGLE, PERTH, FROM THE EPITAPH TO
WILLIAM ANDERSON'S CHILDREN, 1732

The tyrant, Death, spares neither age nor sex,
The gayist mark he haughtily affects;
Parents from children, Husbands from their wives,
He often tears, when most they wish their lives;
Learn then to fix on nothing here belou,
But on thy God, he'll Heaven on the bestou.

FETTERCAIRN, KINCARDINE, ALEXANDER CROLL, 1747

Oh Death! how absolute thy sway!
At thy command we must obey;
In hardy strength 'tis vain to trust
Even stone thou crumblest into dust.

HADDINGTON, EAST LOTHIAN, GEORGE CUNNINGHAM, 1755

THE PHILOSOPHY OF THE MOURNERS

THE TENDER GRSE IT SPRINGS, IT FLOVRS, IT FADES,
THE DAY BEGINS, ASCENS, DECLINES IN SHADES;
FRAIL MANS LIKE GRASE, HIS LIFE A DAY, AND MOST
RVN OVT HIS RACE, AND BE DISOLVED IN DVST.

KINNAIRD, ANGUS, HENRIE RAIT, AGED 18, 1669.

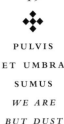

PULVIS
ET UMBRA
SUMUS
*WE ARE
BUT DUST
AND
SHADOWS*

Our life is a flying shaddow,
God is the pol,
The Indings pointing at him is our soul.
Death is the horizin where our sun do set
And through Christ, a resurrection get.

MEIGLE, PERTHSHIRE, DAVID PORTER, 1718

The earth goeth to the earth
Glistring like gold;
The earth goeth to the earth
Sooner than it wold;
The earth builds on the earth
Castles and towers;
The Earth says to the earth
All will be ours.

MELROSE, ROXBURGHSHIRE, — 1761

Our life is but a winter day —
Some only breakfast and away:
Whilst others do to denner stay.
Large is his debt who lingers out the day,
Those who go soonest have the least to pay.

DUNOTTAR, ABERDEEN, JAMES BURLEY, 1783

Death wounds to cure, we fall, we rise, we reign, —
Spring from our fetters fasten in the skies;
Where blooming Eden withers in our sight,
The king of terrors is the prince of peace.

DUMFRIES, MRS MITCHELL, 1792

HEAR IS THE BURIAL PLACE
APPOINTED FOR JOHN
GEDDES GLOVER IN
ELGIN
AND ISOBELL
McKEAN HIS SPOUSE AND
THEIR RELATIONS THIS
WORLD IS A CITIE FULL OF
STREETS DEATH IS YE
MERCAT THAT AL MEN
MEETS IF LIFE WERE A
THING THAT MONIE COULD
BY YE POOR COULD NOT
LIVE & THE RICH WOULD
NAT DIE.

ELGIN CATHEDRAL BURIAL GROUND, MORAY, 1687

COMMENTS FROM THE DEAD

Weep not my wife and children dear,
I am not dead but do sleep here;
My debt is paid, my grave you see,
Therefore prepare and follow me.

CAMPBELLTOWN, ARGYLL, DUNCAN SMITH, 1759

Farewell vain world, I'v had enough of thee,
Now carles what thou sayest of me;
Thy love I court not, nor thy frown I fear,
My days are past, my head lies cover'd here
If fault in me, be sure take care to shun,
Look to yo'rself, for to death you soon must come.

STRATHMARTINE CHURCHYARD, ANGUS,
JAMES BROWN AND HIS SONS, 1795

OPPOSITE.
ELGIN CATHEDRAL
BURIAL GROUND,
MORAY.
JOHN GEDDES GLOVER
AND ISABELL MCKEAN,
1687

GRACE ... FRIEND

MEMENTO MORI

1 · IGR · 87

HEIR IS PE BURIA PLAC
APOINTED FOR IOHN
GEDDES GLOVER BUR
GES IN ELGIN
          AND ISSOBELL
MCREGN HIS SPOUS ·
          & PER RELATO
HIS WORLD IS A CITE
FULL OF STREETS · &
DEATH IS PE PER CAT
PAT ALL PEN MEETS
IF LYFE WERE A PING
PAT MONIE COULD
BUY PE POOR COULD
NOT LIVE S PE RICH
WOULD NOT DIE
S

O mortal man, why dost thow in
This world delight to stay;
And as a drudge by her ay hurled
Even at her fortouns sway?
She's painted our with pleasures rare
All drest in gaudy hue;
She flatter can, without compare,
Yet none of them is true.

INVERGOWRIE, ANGUS, ROBERT COCK AGED NINE YEARS, 1751

Methinks I hear the doolfull passing Bell,
Setting an oneset to its lowder knell;
Methinks I hear my dearest friends lament
With sighs, and tears, and wofull drieryment.
Methinks I see my children standing by,
Vewing the death bed wherupon I ly;
Methinks I hear a voice in secret say —
Thy glass is run, and thou must die today.

INVERKEILOR, ANGUS, ALEXANDER DEAS, 1746

DEATH THE LEVELLER

DEATHS A CALL ALL MORTALS MUST OBEY
AND BY DEATH'S SVMONDS THEY BE CATCHT AVAY,
INTO ANE MINVT, OF THIS VORLD ITS STAGE,
BOTH RICH & POOR, YOVNG & THOSE OF OLD AGE.
THIR PERSONS LIVD IN GREAT FIDELITIE,
BVT NOV THEY PAST INTO ETERNITIE.
THEIR NEIGHBOVRS AND ALL OTHERS DID YM LOVE,
SOE NOV ITS HOPT THEY ARE IN HEAVENS ABOVE

STRACATHRO, ANGUS, DAVID BURNE, DIED 1681,
DAVID BURNE HIS SON DIED 1675

The grave. Great Teacher, to one level brings
Heroes & Beggars, Galley-Slaves, and Kings.

LOCHLEE, ANGUS, DONALD NICOL, 1800

PULVIS
ET UMBRA
SUMUS
*WE ARE
BUT DUST
AND
SHADOWS*

'Tis here the fool, the wise. the low, the high,
In mix'd disorder, and in silence ly;
No more beneath life's weighty load he goes,
But in this chamber finds a quiet repose.
O humbling thought, Pride must be thus disgrac'd,
And all distinctions here at last effac'd.

FARNELL, ANGUS, JOHN BRIMNER, 1791,
BY HIS WIFE HELEN SMITH

All you that walk among the tombs,
Above the silent clay,
Consider how you've spent your time
To fit you for this way.
That mortal man returns to dust,
Experience lets us see;
The high, the low, the rich, the poor,
Must ly as low as me.

MILLPORT, ARGYLL, ERECTED BY JOHN WOOD
IN MEMORY OF HIS FATHER

IN MOURNING

Lo children three, by God's decree,
Dissolving here do ly,
Their tender years with floods of tears,
Lament ought you and I.
Lets cry, alas, all flesh is grass.
Here fades all worldly pleasure:
Let's dart our eyes beyond the skies
And seek for heavenly treasure.

MONIFIETH, ANGUS, FROM THE EPITAPH TO
THE ARCKLAY CHILDREN, 1742

A precious useful Christian here
Sleeps with his pious wife,
Same Sabbath of a different year
Both were bereft of life.
Their daughter young, 'tho cedar tall,
Blends with her parent's dust;
Death then aloud proclaims to all
In youth how vain thy trust.

ORWELL, KINROSS, AR. ER.

PULVIS
ET UMBRA
SUMUS

WE ARE

BUT DUST

AND

SHADOWS

———————— Nor herb, fruit, flow'r
Glistening with dew, nor fragrance after showers;
Nor grateful evening mild, nor walk by moon,
Or glittering star light, without thee is sweet.

DUMFRIES, FROM THE EPITAPH TO PHILADELPHIA, DAUGHTER OF JAMES
DOUGLAS, WHO DIED 6TH FEBRUARY 1754, AGED THIRTY ONE.

Here in one grave tuo lovelie virgins ly,
Tuo sisters dear destined in youth to dy;
Their persons beauty, grace their souls adorn'd,
No wonder then their death is deeply mourn'd.

CRUDEN, ABERDEEN, REBECCA HAY DAUGHTER OF THE REV. MR HAY,
DIED NOVEMBER 1771, AGED 18 YEARS & JEAN HAY DIED JUNE 1772,
AGED 24 YEARS.

All men live in the same Death power,
who seised my beloved man in an hour.
One word to me he could not speak
Though floods of tears ran down his cheek.

MONIFIETH, ANGUS, MARGARET BROWN OF
HER HUSBAND ALEX PATERSON, 1786

OUR FIRST FATHERS

HERE STAND ADAM AND EVE
TREE AND ALL
WHICH BY HIS FALL
WE WERE MADE SINNERS ALL

ST MUNGO, DUMFRIES, JOHN BELL, 1727

Al ye people That paz by
On thez stone youl cast your ey,
Thus was the way that sin began
Woman she beckoned unto man.

METHVEN, PERTH, JOHN WATT, 1748

A GARDINE WE WAS FIRST PUT IN,
TO WORK AND PLAY WE DID BEGINE,
BUT LUSEFAIRE DID US INVAY
AND BROUGHT US TO THIS MISERAY.
THE WAGES OF OUR SIN IS DEATH,
WHICH MAKES ME LIE UPON THIS EARTH,
YET I BELIEVE I SHALL ARYSE
AND MEET MY GOD IN THE SKYES.

ALVA OLD, CLACKMANAN, JM JH MV 1759

ADAM AND EVE, BY EATING OF THE FOBIDDEN TREE
BROUGHT ALL MANKIN'D TO SIN AND MISERY.
THE MARRIAGE OF THE SOUL AND CHRIST
NO DEATH DISOLVE IT CAN
BUT CARNALL MARRIAGES IT MAYE
OF WIFE AND OF THE MAN.

STRACATHRO, ANGUS, MARY SYMMER WIFE OF
JOHN TINDAL, AGED 30, 1782

❖

OPPOSITE.
JOHN WATT,
THE MASON,
WEARING HIS APRON
HEADS THE STONE,
AND HIS TOOLS OF
TRADE, ENCIRCLED,
ARE BALANCED BY
A SCENE OF THE
TEMPTATION
WITH THE SERPENT
COILED ROUND THE
TRUNK OF THE
APPLE TREE.
METHVEN, PERTH,
1748.

BY SAD CHANCE

The penetrating art of man,
Unfold this secret never can,
How long men shall live on the Earth,
And how, or where give up their Breath.
The person of whom this I write,
Ah! dy'd by a mournfull fate;
An old clay chimney that downfell,
Kill'd both servant and himsell,
Which should alarm men every where
For their last hour well to prepare,
That death may never them surprise;
For as the tree falls, so it lies.

KIRKDEN, ANGUS, ROBERT ALEXANDER, 1738

Stop traveller as you go by,
I once had life and breath;
But falling from a steeple high
I swiftly passed through death.

JEDBURGH, ROXBURGH, JAMES HUNTER, WRIGHT, 1765

OPPOSITE.
ST QUIVOX,
AYRSHIRE,
JAMES MCALL,
+1766,
SHOWS A UNIQUE
VERSION OF ADAM
AND EVE LEAVING
PARADISE. THE
STONE IS FLAKING.
THE INSCRIPTION
WAS 'ON THE DAY
THOU EATEST OF IT
THOU SHALT DIE'

In memory of David Greig;
his age was 28, death sudden,
on the sea beach at Aberdeen.

Young and sprightly lads as you pass by
Stop and review how low I lie;
My colleague fell close by my side.
At nine we were as brisk as ye,
At ten were in eternity;
Swept by a strong refluent tide,
I twenty eight, he twenty four,
One fatal wave did us devour.

GLENBERVIE, KINCARDINE, DAVID GREIG. 1818

Ye little children that survey,
The emblem'd wheel that crush'd me down,
Be cautious as you careless play,
For shafts of death fly thick around.

KILMARNOCK, AYRSHIRE, ROBERT WEBSTER, 1809

HERE LYES FRANCES
ARMSTRANG SON TO
WILLIAM ARMSTRANG
IN GLENYEIR WHO
DIED IN THE WATER
ON THE LORD'S DAY N
OV 2 1696 AS HE WENT
FROM THE KIRK AFTE
R SERMON AGE 28

CANONBIE, DUMFRIES, FRANCES ARMSTRANG, 1696

The church stands near the river, and presumably he crossed by boat.

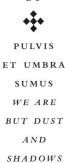

PULVIS
ET UMBRA
SUMUS
*WE ARE
BUT DUST
AND
SHADOWS*

OPPOSITE.
KELLS,
KIRKCUDBRIGHTSHIRE,
AGNES HERESE, 1701.
THIS IS ONE OF
FOUR SIMILAR, BUT
NOT IDENTICAL,
RENDERINGS OF THE
FALL OF MAN
IN THIS CHURCHYARD.
EVE IS SHOWN ON
LEFT OF THE TREE.

LEFT.
CANONBIE
CHURCHYARD,
DUMFRIES. FRANCIS
ARMSTRONG,
1696

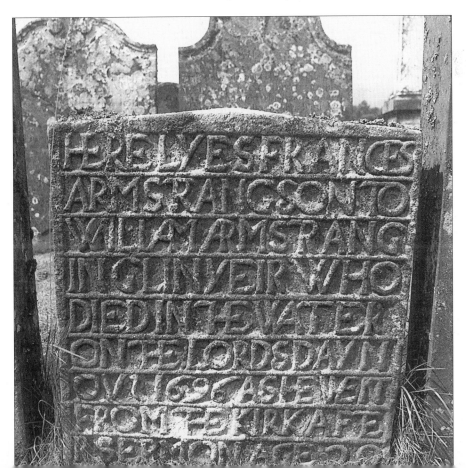

IN
LOVING MEMORY OF MAGGIE
McINTOSH WHO WAS
ACCIDENTLY KILLED IN
LOVE STEWART & Co Nº9
WOODYARD BO'NESS 10TH
JULY 1907 AGED 14 YEARS
A TOKEN OF RESPECT FROM
HER FELLOW WORKERS.

From what befalls us here below,
Let none from thence conclude,
Our lot shall aftertime be so —
The young man's life was good.
Yet Heavenly wisdom thought it fit,
In its all sovereign way,
The flame to kill him to permit,
And so to close his day

LOCHLEE, ANGUS, DANIEL CHRISTISON, AGED 36, 1751

Christison was accidentally burned to death among a quantity of heather.

IN
LOVING MEMORY OF MAGGIE
McINTOSH WHO WAS
ACCIDENTALLY KILLED IN
LOVE STEWART & CO No 9
WOODYARD BO'NESS 10TH
JULY 1907 AGED 14 YEARS
A TOKEN OF RESPECT FROM
HER FELLOW WORKERS.

CARRIDEN, WEST LOTHIAN, MAGGIE McINTOSH, 1907

PULVIS
ET UMBRA
SUMUS
*WE ARE
BUT DUST
AND
SHADOWS*

OPPOSITE.
MANY OF THE
CAST-IRON
MONUMENTS
WHICH APPEARED
IN THE NINETEENTH
CENTURY HAVE
RUSTED OR BEEN
DISPLACED. THIS
ONE IS OF UNIQUE
DESIGN. CARRIDEN,
WEST LOTHIAN,
MAGGIE McINTOSH,
1907

ROXBURGH
CHURCHYARD,
ROXBURGHSHIRE,
JAMES HEWAT,
+1745

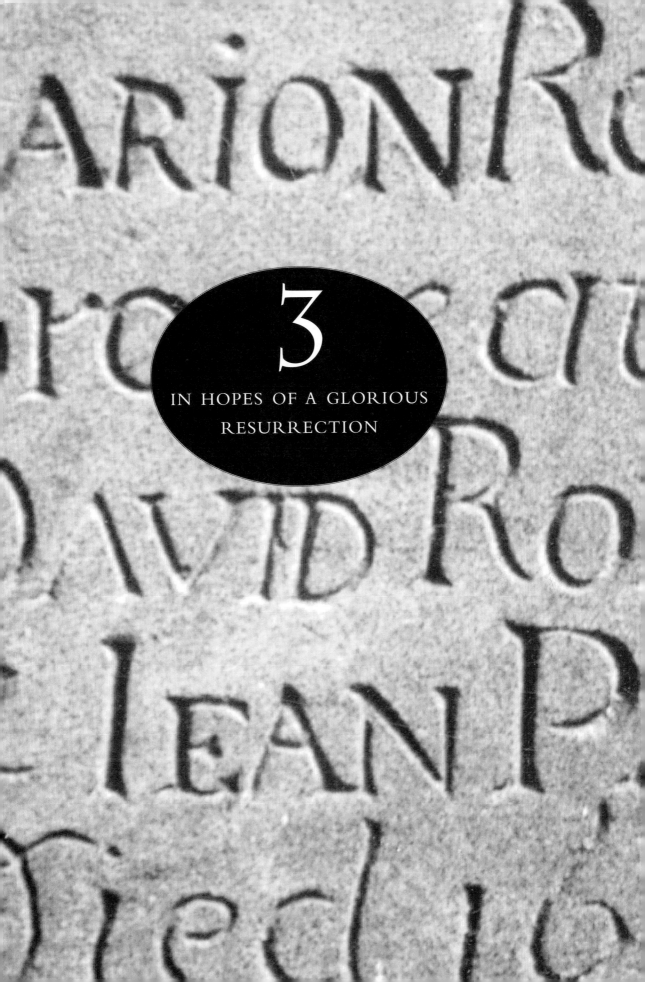

3

IN HOPES OF A GLORIOUS
RESURRECTION

Just as the skull and bones were the most popular emblems which signified death, so the winged head took its place on most monuments to signify the Resurrection. It represents the soul of the deceased, which at the moment of death leaves the body and soars up into the Heavens. There it waits for the Day of Judgement, when, at the call of the trumpets, it arises clothed in new flesh to join the soul. In North America it is often called the soul effigy.

In Italian Renaissance art, cherubims, in the guise of winged heads, were used to signify the souls of the Blessed; this image was adopted after the Reformation to signify the soul in funerary art. Many of the winged heads on English gravestones are similar to the faces of the putti (cherubs in Italian Renaissance art); child-like, innocent, plump and pretty. But in Scotland and in New England, where religious fervour was stronger, there was more concern in portraying the message. In addition the masons strived to make each stone individual. There are as many variations in the soul effigies as one might see in the faces of a great gathering of people. Although the soul was anonymous, sexless, and ageless, the depictions of them on the seventeenth and eighteenth century stones have not turned out as such. Some of the putti faces are on memorials to children, but others relate to adults and even to old people. The majority of souls, whether on stones to young, middle-aged or old people, have expressions which range from intense, grim, lugubrious, severe, to purposeful, serene, jolly or joyful. The customer may on a whim have chosen to have one, two, or even three soul effigies.

Hairstyles may be according to the period, or are sometimes periwigs or full wigs. Some have bald heads, some masses of curls or long hair. The wing structures vary greatly in position; in composition they are usually modelled on those of birds, but may be leaf-like; they vary considerably in style.

Angels of the Resurrection appear blowing on trumpets; they are usual robed and in flight. Occasionally they are depicted as winged heads blowing trumpets. Resurrection scenes may take the form of a trumpeting angel arousing the skeleton of the deceased, or of a naked figure ascending skywards. The sometimes primitive folk art makes a strong impact; these carvings and the biblical quotations and the epitaphs put over the message of the Church: in the Westminster Confession of Faith it is stated that 'the bodies of men, after death, return to the dust and see corruption; but their souls (which neither die not or sleep) having an immortal substance, immediately return toGod who gave them'. Various emblems were carved to represent the hope of eternal life, so often expressed in epitaphs which were to comfort the bereaved, but more importantly to warn the living to do good and seek grace. Depictions of the Tree of Life, greenery such as palm fronds and wreaths, cornucopia, crowns, flaming torches spoke as clearly as the words inscribed on the tombs.

PREVIOUS PAGE.
DETAIL.
POLMONT
CHURCHYARD,
MARION ROBERTSON,
+1734

OPPOSITE.
ANCRUM OLD
CHURCHYARD,
ROXBURGHSHIRE,
BETTY BOWER, N.D.
A BEAUTIFUL
EXAMPLE OF A
WINGED SOUL
CARVED IN HIGH
RELIEF.

THOSE SOULS THOSE DEATHLESS THINGS

His soul breathed upward, and at last
Arrived above, the mantle's here downcast

EASSIE, ANGUS, THE REVEREND DAVID ADAMSON, 1720

When nature first my slender body fram'd
Within a living grave of dust enchain'd,
She destin'd me that I at last should have
And change this mortal for a living grave.
But tho' my body in this Urn doth rest,
In small & scattered particles disperst;
My soul, that Heavenly Substance, and divine
Hath soar'd aloft into its native clime.

FOULIS EASTER, PERTH, FROM THE EPITAPH TO AGNES BEIG, 1766

MEIGLE,
PERTHSHIRE,
WILLIAM WATSON,
1762. TWO
TRUMPETING ANGELS
SUMMON THE DEAD
FROM THE GRAVE.

As Heaven decreed, we've all agreed
That soul and body sever,
Eerth to the clod
The soul to God
Shal live and reign forever.

MONIFIETH, ANGUS, FROM THE EPITAPH TO
THE ARCKLAY CHILDREN, 1742

Beneath this stone in silent slumber sleeps
Her sacred dust, whose soul sweet Jesus keeps;
Which wing'd its way thro' ether's regions high,
To be united with saints above the sky;
In piety with virtue bright she shone,
A tender mother, wife and friend in one;
Lamented death, those children dear did cost
Husband grief for what they had, and lost.

ANNAN, DUMFRIES, BARBARA STEWART SPOUSE TO JOHN ROOM, WHO
DIED 1730, LEAVING BEHIND HER SIX CHILDREN.

Be thou faithful unto Death and I
will give thee a crown of Life
An honest and an upright man
Resolved to dust here lys,
His soul by Faith in Jesus blood
Now soars above the Skys.
When Christ his Lord in Glory comes
To his compleat Salvation,
His dust shall quicken into Life
At the great Consummation.

MEIGLE, PERTHSHIRE, WILLIAM WATSON, 1762

THE TRUMPETS SHALL SOUND
AND THE DEAD SHALL ARISE

The trumpets shall sound
the dead shall arise
to meet Christ Jesus
Above the skies

LOGIEPERT, ANGUS, THE BUCHANAN STONE, 1737.

Here lies three Hopes enclos'd within,
Death's prisoners by Adam's sin,
Yet rest in hope that they shall be
Set by the second Adam free.

ST ANDREWS, PEEBLES, THOMAS HOPE, LATE TREASURER IN PEEBLES,
HIS WIFE AND CHILDREN, LATE SEVENTEENTH CENTURY

TOP.

THE BUCHANAN

STONE, 1737.

LOGIEPERT, ANGUS

BELOW.

BO'NESS,

WEST LOTHIAN

THE ONLY

INSCRIPTION IS

JP CB, 1763.

THE STRANGE

SYMBOLIC CARVINGS

SPEAK OF

DEATH AND

RESURRECTION.

Like to the seed in earthy womb,
Or like dead Lazarus in the tomb,
Or like Tabitha in a sleep,
Or Jonas like within the deep,
Or like the moon or stars in day,
Ly hid and lanquish quite away;
Even as the grave the dead receives.
Man being dead he death deceives.
The seed springs, and Lazarus stands,
Tabitha wakes, and Jonas lands;
The moon appears, and stars remain,
So man being dead shall live again.

RESCOBIE, ANGUS, JOHN ESPLINE, 1717

and the dead shall rise to meet Christ Jesus

ME·ME·NTO·MORI

EPITAPHS
AND IMAGES
FROM
SCOTTISH
GRAVEYARDS

TOP.
A DETAIL
FROM A
TABLESTONE.
MURROES, ANGUS,
ALEAXANDER
EDWARDS, 1655.
THE ROW OF
SUPPLIANT FIGURES
HAVE RISEN
FROM THE GRAVE.

BELOW.
KINKELL OLD
CHURCHYARD,
ABERDEEN
THOMAS TANNER,
1759.
THIS STONE HAS
A CONFUSED AND
RARE IMAGE — AN
ANGEL WHO CARRIES
THE SCYTHE OF DEATH
ON THE SINISTER
SIDE, AND ALSO
THE TRIUMPHANT
TRUMPET OF THE
RESURRECTION.

I, when the Trumpet Sounds with joy,
Shall quit my earthly bed;
The voice that calls me wont annoy —
Arise, come forth ye Dead.

MARYTON, ANGUS, JAMES PETRIE, 1789

Hail! happy soul, thy race is safely run,
Thy sorrows ended, and thy joys begun;
Thy sacred dust in sweet repose shall keep,
Till Heaven's last trumpet rouse oblivion sleep.
Then fresh renewed thy sacred dust shall rise,
Re-assume its form, and hail its native skies.
Of love and duty this last pledge receive —
It's all thy parents thee survives can give.

DAVIOT, INVERNESSHIRE, JOHN, SON OF WILLIAM PAUL
AND MARGARET BRUCE, DIED 1794, AGED 19½ YEARS

Til Heaven and earth wrapped in a scrol shall be
And Christ with saints coming in the clouds ile se,
When soule and bodies united shall againe
Be lifted up to Christ for to reamine.

STRATHMARTINE, ANGUS, ISOBEL MATHEW

If I be wicked, woe unto me; and if I be righteous,
yet will I not lift up mine head. I am full of confusion;
therefore see thou mine affliction.

JOB X V. 15
MURROES, ANGUS, ALEXANDER EDWARDS, 1655

OPPOSITE.
KIRKMICHAEL,
AYRSHIRE,
ARTHUR FULTON,
1739.
THE ANGEL WITH
TWO ACOLYTES
SPEAKS POWERFULLY
OF THE HOPE
OF HEAVEN.

LEFT.
MOCHRUM,
WIGTOWNSHIRE,
JOHN LEYBURN, 1739.
THE SAINTLY IMAGE
OF JOHN LEYBURN,
MASON, HAS ANGEL
HEADS TRUMPETING
IN EITHER EAR,
A CROWN OF
EVERLASTING LIFE
ON HIS HEAD, AND
THE EMBLEMS OF
DEATH. THE NAKED
RESURRECTION
FIGURE STANDS ON
A FOLIATE HEAD.

4

EULOGIES TO LOVED
ONES

Friends, Romans, countrymen, lend me your ears
I come to bury Caesar, not to praise him,
The evil that men do lives after them,
The good is often interred with their bones.

Thus begins Mark Antony's funeral oration to Caesar. Strange, when considered in isolation, for the observance of 'De mortuis nihil bonum' was generally accepted. But Mark Antony began with these arresting lines which lead on to a triumph of sardonic invective.

Nevertheless, there is something in us which revolts against too fulsome praise in a seemingly endless eulogy. We begin to think about the human foibles which were dear, and to question unadulterated praise. Many Scots thought the best epitaph was HERE LYES ANE HONEST MAN — the same prime virtue was also occasionally given to women. Simplicity appeals, as in the epitaph to Janet Dryburgh at West Wemyss, Fife, who died in 1768.

'Underneath this stone doth ly
as much vertue as could die'

With the Renaissance came the custom of inscribing long eulogies on the tombs of the nobility and the great. To some extent this fashion was continued on churchyard tombs, though the length was limited by the available money and space on the tomb. Eulogising went to ridiculous lengths, as in this instance which appeared at Greyfriars, Edinburgh:

Alexander Monteith, druggist in Edinburgh, a
man remarkably distinguished by true greatness
of soul, and by far the most eminent in the surgical
art — whose sepulchral mound might be termed a
pile of virtues, the lofty eulogies upon which,
pronounced on the non-professional, and contained
in all the foregoing epitaphs, unless they were
confined within their own lines and limits,
having formed themselves into a phlanx [sic]
would pass over and through force of kin, would
emulously rush in and fly in troops to him —— [etc.!]
He departed this life on December 23rd 1713,
two days before the festival of the birth
of Christ, lest the mourning and the sadness
on account of the decease of the former might
interrupt the joy and exultation of the nativity
of the latter.

PREVIOUS PAGE.
DETAIL, ANWOTH,
KIRKCUDBRIGHTSHIRE,
CHRISTEN,
LADY CARDYNE,
1628

OPPOSITE.
GREYFRIARS BURIAL
GROUND,
THE PETERS FAMILY,
+1753

How different from the moving lines of Robert Louis Stevenson which are more telling and more moving than many a eulogising epitaph.

> Under the wide and starry sky,
> Dig the grave and let me lie.
> Glad did I live and gladly die,
> And I laid me down with a will.
> This be the verse your grave for me
> Here he lies where he wished to be;
> Home is the sailor, home from the sea,
> And the hunter home from the hill.

We may well pause here and consider how many famous Scots found fame and graves far from their native land. The selection of eulogies — particularly those for famous men, is small; were it otherwise it might be tedious, there being a limited number of virtues to extol. Most of them are a reminder of the suffering of the bereaved — but the comfort brought in the expression of their feelings. A high proportion of the churchyard monuments were erected to children and the words, often quaintly expressed, are of sincerity, sadness, of loss and yet of hope.

LET US NOW PRAISE FAMOUS MEN

Mural monument, John Milne, Greyfriars Burial Ground, Edinburgh 1667. John Milne, sixth kings master-mason of the race of Milne, exquisitly skilful of the architectonick art, of times Deacon Conveener of the trades of Edinburgh, the circumspect and faithful representative of the Metropolis and several times commissioner to the Parliament for the metropolitan; considerate and faithful; a man adorned with gifts of the mind above his degree; of a comely stature of body, good, courageous, Godly, and to be esteemed by all, died 1667.

> Great artesan, grave senator, John Milne,
> Renown'd for learning, prudence, parts and skill,
> Who in his life, Vitruvius art had shown,
> Adorning others' monuments: his own
> Can have no other beauty, than his name,
> His memory and everlasting fame.
> Rare man he was, who could unite, in one,
> Highest and lowest occupation;
> To sit with statesmen, councillour to kings,
> To work with tradesmen, in mechanick things;
> Majestick man, for person, witt and grace;
> This generation cannot fill his place.

The first part is translated from Latin by Weever; the verse is in English.

STATED BY PETTIGREW TO HAVE BEEN ON THE TOMB
OF ROBERT FERGUSSON, AT THE CANONGATE, EDINBURGH

To the Memory of
ROBERT BURNS, the Ayrshire Bard;
who was born at Doonside,
On the 29th January 1759
and died at Dumfries
On the 22nd of July, 1796.
O ROBBIE BURNS, the Man, the Brither
And art thou gone, — and gone for ever;
And hast thou crossed that unknown river,
Life's dreary bound?
Like thee, where shall we find anither
The world around ?
Go to your sculptur'd tombs, ye Great,
In a' the tinsel trash o' state;
But by the honest turf I'll wait,
Thou man of worth,
And weep the sweetest poet's fate,
E'er lived on earth.

FROM THOMAS BANNATYNE'S MONUMENT,
GREYFRIARS, EDINBURGH, 1635

Today is mine, tomorrow yours may be;
Each mortal man should mind, that he must die.
What is man's life? a shade, a smoak, a flower,
Short to the good; to th' bad, doth long endure.
If thou list, that passeth by,
Know, who in this tomb doth ly;
Thomas Bannatyne, abroad
And at home who served GOD.
Though no children he possest,
Yet the Lord with means him blest,
He on them did well dispose,
Long ere death his eyes did close.
For, the poor his helping hand,
And his friends with kindness fand.
He died in July 1635 and of age, 65

O that men
were wise, to $\left\{\rule{0pt}{7em}\right.$ Know the multitude of these that are
to be damned; the paucity of those that
are to be saved; and the vanity
of transitory things.
Understand evil committed, good
things omitted, and the loss of time.
Foresee the danger of death, the last
judgement, and eternal punishment.

COLLAPSED FINIAL
OF THE THOMAS
BANNATYNE TOMB.
GREYFRIARS,
EDINBURGH.
NOTE THE
TALL 'APARTMENT
BLOCK' BUILDING IN
THE BACKGROUND,
WITH A DEATH'S
HEAD PEERING OUT
OF ONE WINDOW.
THESE EARLY
MURAL MONUMENTS
AT GREYFRIARS
ARE CLEARLY THE
WORK OF SUPERIOR
MASONS.

ST ANDREWS CATHEDRAL BURIAL GROUND, FIFE, MR SAMUELL RUTHERFORD
WHO DIED 1661 (RENEWED HEADSTONE, EPITAPH RECUT)

Here lyes the Reverend M. Samuell Rutherford
Professor of Divinity in the University of St Andrews
What tongu! what Pen, or Skill of Men,
Can Famous Rutherford commend,
His Learning justly raisd his Fame,
True GODliness adorn'd His Name.
He did converse with things Above,
Acquainted with Emmanuel's love.
Most orthodox He was and sound,
And Many Errors did confound.
For Zion's King and Zion's cause
And Scotland's covenanted LAWS
Most constantly he Did contend
Until his Time was At An End.
Than he wan to the Full Fruition
Of That which He Had seen in vision.

GREYFRIARS, EDINBURGH, GEORGE HERIOT, GOLDSMITH, BURGESS
TO THE CITY, AND JEWELLER TO THE TWO RENOWNED PRINCES K. JAMES VI
AND K. CHARLES, 1610 TRANSLATED FROM LATIN

Passenger, who art wise, hence know whence you are,
What you are, and what you are to be,
Life, gate of death; death, gate of life, to me;
Sole death of death gives life eternallie.
Therefore, whoever breath draws from the air,
While live thou mayst, thyself for death prepare.

RHU, DUNBARTONSHIRE, HENRY BELL, +1830

In Memory of
HENRY BELL
who died on the 14th of November 1830
The Comet, built for Henry Bell in 1811
was the first steam vessel in Europe
which successfully navigated rivers and
open seas

THE GOOD, THE TRUE, THE BRAVE, THE JUST

FROM HAWICK CHURCHYARD AND NOW IN THE MUSEUM, WALTER SCOT, 1596

VALTER SCOT OF GOVDILANDIS HIS QUALITIES
HERE LYIS BVRIT VISDOME & VIRTHINES
HERE LYIS BVREIT TREVTH & HONESTIE,
HERE LYES BVREIT FRIDOME & GENTRES
HERE LYIS BVREIT MANHEID AND CHERITIE
HERE LYIS BVREIT LAIRGENESS & LAVTIE
HERE LYIS BVREIT HAP & EXPRIENCE
HERE LYIS BVREIT PIETIE & DILIGENCE
GLORIE BE TO GOD FOR AL THINGS.

GREYFRIARS BURIAL GROUND, PERTH, JOHN CONQUEROR, WHO DIED 1653

O'ER DEATH A CONQUEROR HE NOW
LYES WHOSE SOULE,
FREED FROM HIS DUST, TRIUMPHES ABOVE
THE POLE.
ONE LESS THAN TWYCE TWELVE CHILDREN
BY ONE WIFE
HE HAD, OF WHICH TO EVERLASTING LIFE
TWYCE TEN HE SENT BEFORE HIM,
AND BEHYND
HE LEFT BUT THREE TO PROPOGATE HIS KYND.
HE RAN TEN LUSTRES OUT, WHEN RIGID FATE
ROBBED HIM OF LIFE, PERTH OF A MAGISTRATE.

RHU,
DUMBARTONSHIRE,
HENRY BELL,
+1830

LOGIE-MAR CHURCHYARD, ABERDEEN, DONALD GORDON, 1776, AGED 98

Altho' this tomb no boasted tittles keep
Yet silent here the private virtues sleep;
Truth, candour, justice, altogether ran
And form'd a plain, upright, honest man.

LOCHLEE, ANGUS, FROM THE EPITAPH TO CHARLES GARDEN,
DIED 1781 AGED 90

Entomb'd here lies what's mortal of the man,
Who fill'd with honour Life's extended span;
Of stature handsome, front erect amd fair,
Of dauntless brow, yet mild and debonair.
. . . .
He was the Husband, Father, Neighbour, Friend,
And all their special properties sustain'd,
Of prudent conduct, and of morals sound,
And who at last with length of days was crown'd.

ALLOWAY,
AYRSHIRE,
JAMES BURNESS,
1777

ALLOWAY, AYRSHIRE, ROBERT BURNS' EPITAPH TO
HIS FATHER JAMES BURNES, 1777

O YE whose cheek the tear of pity stains,
Draw near with pious reverence and attend!
Here lie the loving husband's dear remains,
The tender father and the gen'rous friend:
The pitying heart that felt for human woe!
The dauntless heart that fear's no human pride!
The friend of man, to vice alone a foe.
For e'v'n his failings lean'd to virtue's side.

TWO MEN OF LARBERT, A CONTRAST OF STYLES

LARBERT, STIRLING, JOHN BURN, 1665

HERE LYES INTERRED WITHIN THIS URN,
THE CORPSE OF HONEST GOOD JOHN BURN,
WHO WAS THE EIGHT JOHN OF THAT NAME,
WHO LIVED WITH LOVE AND DIED WITH FAME.
IN CHANGING TYMES, SADDEST DISASTER,
TRUE TO HIS KING, LORD AND MASTER!
KIND TO HIS KINDRED, NEIGHBOUR, FRIEND,
WHO'S GOOD LYFE HAD AN HAPPIE END,
HIS SOUL TO GOD HE DID BEQUEATH
HIS DUST, TO LYE THIS STONE BENEATH.

LARBERT, STIRLING, JAMES BRUCE ESQ. OF KINNAIRD, 1794

His life was spent in performing useful and
splendid actions; he explored many distant regions,
he discovered the fountains of the Nile, he traversed
the deserts of Nubia. He was an affectionate husband,
an indulgent parent, an ardent lover of his country.
By the unanimous voice of mankind, his name
is enrolled with those who were conspicuous for
genius, for valour, and for virtue.

ON VERTUOUS WOMEN

RECORDED AS OUTSIDE ST GILES CHURCH, EDINBURGH,
ANNA FOULLER, WHO DIED 1645, AGED 48

TWO VERT'OUS HANDS, ONE TRUTH-EXPRESSING TONGUE,
A FURNISHT HEART, WITH PIETY, FAITH, AND LOVE,
A FRUITFUL WOMB, WHENCE HOPEFUL MALES ARE SPRUNG,
TWO LUST-FREE EYES, THOUGHTS TENDING FAR ABOVE
THE REACH OF NATURE, MOTIONLESS BECOME,
REST PEACEABLY INTO THIS EARTHLY TOMB.

ANWOTH, KIRKCUDBRIGHTSHIRE, CHRISTEN, LADY CARDYNE, 1628

ZE.GAIZERS.ON.THIS.TROPHEE.OF.A.TOMBE,
SEND.OVT.ONE.GRONE.FOR. WANT.OF.HIR.WHOIS.LYFE
TWYSE.BORNE.ON.EARTH.AND.NOW.IS.IN.EARTHIS.WOMBE,
LIVED.LONG.A.VIRGINE.NOW.A.SPOTLES.WIFE.
CHVRCH.KEEPS.HIR.GODLIE.LIFE.THIS.TOMBE.HIR.CORPS
AND.EARTH.HIR.FAMOVS.NAME.
WHO.THEN.DOES.LOSE?.HIR.HVSBAND.NO.SINCE.HEAVEN
HIR.SAVLE.DOES.GAINE.CHRISTEN.MAKCADDAM.LADY
CARDYNES.DEPAIRTED.16.IVNY.1628.AETATIS.SVAE.33.

ANWOTH,
KIRKCUDBRIGHTSHIRE,
CHRISTEN,
LADY CARDYNE,
1628.
SEE DETAIL ON
PAGE 47

ST ANDREWS CATHEDRAL, (TRANSLATED FROM LATIN)

In this little grave is enclosed a most singular woman,
Judith Nairn, most beloved spouse to John Weems
merchant, who died December 11th 1646
and of her age 80.

Eternal seeds of all things rise again,
All dead things fall to earth, and there remain:
Candour, faith, goodness, virtue, justice true
And constant piety here engrossed are.

The gravestone (above) shows a scene from Quarles Emblems Book 1V, X1, 'I
will arise and go about the city, and will seek him whom my soul loveth: I
sought him, but I found him not. Canticles iii.2. There is a head behind the
bed drapes, which, in the book illustration, has a halo, and signifies Christ.

MARYKIRK, ANGUS, THE THORNTON AISLE, 1661

A funeral song to the memory of the most excellent woman
Dame Edith Forbes, Lady of Thornton, who, possessed of
all the merits that can adorn her sex, became a candidate

ST ANDREWS
CATHEDRAL
MUSEUM, FIFE,
JUDITH NAIRN,
1667, DETAIL

for eternity 10th January 1661, in the 25th year of her
age, having died prematurely in childbed. This monument
was erected by her sorrowing husband.
one who was lately a light to her country now flits an
unsubstantial shadow. If the golden dawn showed so bright
a light with what splendour would the noontide have shone?
— a phoenix she both livd and died, such as ten ages
could not reproduce. But she died ripe for Heaven: what
more was needed? The slothful reckon age, good men deeds.
Death itself shall not part us.

BALQUHIDDER, PERTH, ISABEL CAMPBELL, SPOUSE OF MR ROBERT KIRK, 168

Stones weep tho' eyes are dry,
Choicest flowers soonest die;
Their sun oft sets at noon
Whose fruit is ripe in June.
Then years of joy be thine,
Since earth must soon resign
To God what is divine.

CAERLAVEROCK, DUMFRIES, (ANON), 1730

Scarce will an age afford such one
So prudent, wise and rare,
Pious, humble, modest, meek and wise,
Loadstone-like, attractive, swete.

ALFORD, ABERDEEN, JEAN WISHART, DIED 1759

Here lys below this stons
Pious, Virtus, JEAN WISHART'S bons,
Wife to John Bain
Some time in Bridgend
Of Knockandoch.
All that was dicent & descret,
Did in her parts & in her person meet;
She mead apper thro her unbilemesh'd Life,
The tender & the loving wife.

ST FILLANS, FORGAN, FIFE, THE WIFE OF DAVID SMITH, 1816

A Rachel's beauty, Dorcas open heart,
A Martha's care and Mary's better part
In her were all combined,
Her spirit fled from earth to heaven,
Her body to the dust is given.
Both shall be join'd.

BARRY, ANGUS, SUSAN GIBSON WHO DIED 1835, AGED 29

She was — but words are wanting
To say what —
Think what a wife should be —
She was that.

❖

ST MONANS, FIFE, AGNES GRAY, WIFE OF MR BARRON OF BARRON HALL, 1851

Her excellence indeed to all
Was so brilliant and rare,
That very few in social life
Could once with her compare.

❖

MAN AND WIFE

THE HOWFF BURIAL GROUND, DUNDEE, N.D.

Into thien hands Lord we commit
Our soules which ar thy deue
For why? Thou hast redimed them
O Lord our God most trau

❖

THE HOWFF
BURIAL GROUND,
DUNDEE, ANGUS,
—N.D.

DUN, ANGUS, JOHN ERSKINE & AGNES BURN, 1696

They lived like turtles
and died together, she 1st
May aged 25 and he 15th
April 1696 aged 28

TEVIOTHEAD, ROXBURGHSHIRE, ADAM ROBSON AND JEAN BEATIE, +1760

Here lyes Adam Robson
he died at Karshope
April the 24th 1760 aged 70
Also Jean Beatie spouse to
said Adam. She died April
the 22nd 1755 aged 65

Adam wears a wig and the long jacket of the time, and Jean has a cap on her head. There are a number of similar portrait stones at Castleton and Ettleton.

PITSLIGO, ABERDEEN, ALEXANDER GILL & BARBARA URQUHART, 1742

One Joy we Joy'd, one griefe we griev'd;
One love we lov'd, one life we liv'd;
One was ye hand, one was ye word
That did his death, her death afford
As all the rest, so now the stone
That tombs them two, is Justly one.

DUMFRIES, THOMAS MOUAT, WIGMAKER AND HIS WIFE, 1735

Two lovers true for ten years space absented
By stormy seas and wars, yet liv'd contented; -
We met for eighteen years and married were,
God smil'd on us, our wind blew always fair;
We're anchor'd here waiting our master's call,
Expecting with him joys perpetual.

MOFFAT, DUMFRIES, WILLIAM MUIR AND KATHERINE HIS SPOUSE,
BOTH DIED ANNO DOM. 1759; SHE, NOVEMBER 6; HE, DECEMBER 4

Here lies the man, the woman here,
Their mutual love so passing dear,
When down she in the grave did ly,
Here he reclin'd of sympathy.

BROUGHTY FERRY OLD, ANGUS,
GEORGE CAITHNESS & AGNES LYALL, 1801

They were a couple good without pretence,
Bless'd with plain reason. and with sober sense;
Pride to them unknown, while they drew breath,
Lovely in their lives, undivided in their death.

IN LOVING MEMORY
OF PRINCESS TITANA MARAMA
OF TAHITI
BORN AT PAPETUIA MOCREA
20 NOVEMBER 1842
WIFE OF
GEORGE DAIRSIE
DIED AT ANSTRUTHER
SEPTEMBER 1891

The sea captain brought his bride back to his home in Anstruther, and there treated her as befitted royalty over the happy years of their marriage.

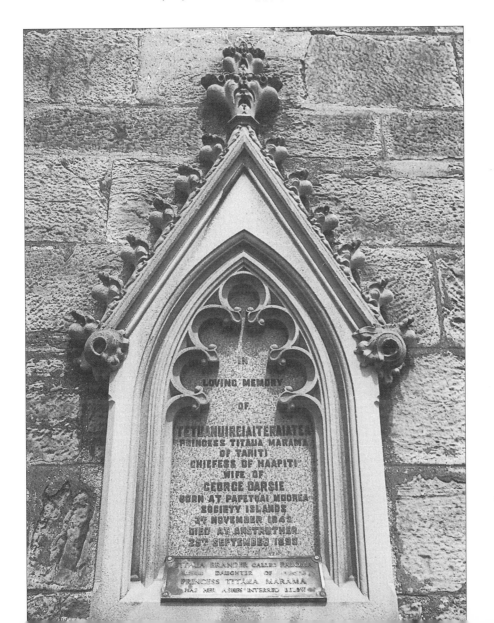

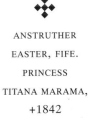

EPITAPHS
AND IMAGES
FROM
SCOTTISH
GRAVEYARDS

GREYFRIARS, EDINBURGH, FRANCISCA SWINTOUN, AGED 7 (N.D.)

The sweetest children are but like fair flow'rs
Which please the fancy for some days and hours;
They soon spring up, but ere they be well grown,
They fade away, their place is no more known:
Only their death, sure, leaveth such a smart,
That grief's engraven on the parent's heart.

STRAITON, AYR, THE LOGAN CHILDREN, JAMES, DAVID, JOHN, THOMAS,
WILLIAM, JEAN, ANNE, JEAN (N.D.)

Six sons, three daughters of a family
Here waiting for the joyful day
The flowers, soon cropped, shall be
made fresh again, the leaves
of Spring, so fresh and gay,
are fallen — the root doth stay;
With voices renewed again to notes more high
in the celestial lightsome choir . . .

STRAITON,
AYRSHIRE,
THE LOGAN
CHILDREN. N.D.

TRANENT, EAST LOTHIAN, JOHN MILL, 1693

Here layes John
Mill son to John
Mill who dyed
1693 aged —

ST VIGEANS, ANGUS, ISOBEL BEWS & HELEN CARGILL, 1744

This stone was set here by
John Cargill residentor in
Seatoun of Auchmithy in memory
of Isobel Bews his Spouse who departed this life the
20 of August 1743 aged 56 years & Helen Cargil third
daughter who Departed this life the 20 of January
1748 at whose head this stone and for whom
the same was designed before the Mother's death

Decay of Nature without regard to age
Hath torn this youthful beauty from of the stage
How frail it is and in hov short a time
It fades like roses when they're past their prime.
We that survive shooner or later must.
Her corpse lyes here now crumbling into dust
While her better part Triumphs above
The highest reach of any human love
And left behind within this silent bed
As fine a girl as ever Corner bred

STOBO, PEEBLES-SHIRE, THE THOMSON SISTERS, 1723

HERE LYES ELIZABETH THOM
SON WHO DIED THE 4 OF MAY
1723 HER AGE 21. AS ALSO
AGNES THOMSON WHO DIED THE
4 OF AUGUST 1723 HER AGE
19. AS ALSO ELIZABETH THOM
SON WHO DIED NOVR 1723
HER AGE 12 YEARS.

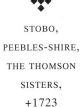

STOBO,
PEEBLES-SHIRE,
THE THOMSON
SISTERS,
+1723

MARJORY FLEMING
"PET MARJORIE"
died at Kirkcaldy
December 19th 1811
aged 8 years and
11 months
"The Youngest Immortal
in The World of Letters"

❖❖

ABBOTSHALL
CHURCHYARD,
KIRKCALDY, FIFE,
MARJORIE FLEMING,
1811

MARJORIE FLEMING
PET MARJORIE
died at Kirkcaldy
December 19th 1811
aged 8 years and
11 months
The youngest Immortal
in the world of letters.

'Pet Marjorie' was a youthful prodigy and a pet of Sir Walter Scott. She wrote a quaint diary, a poem on Mary Queen of Scots, and other verses, and she was the subject of an essay by Dr John Brown.

ORWELL, KINROSS, THE BROWN CHILDREN, 1758

FIVE CHILDRENS dust lyes buried in this place
Their names this mournfull stone doe grace,
JEAN ISABELL LILLIAS JOHN & ROBERT BROWNS
Fair flowers by death soon Blasted all down,
Dear lovely Souls! on earth short was thy stay.
They smile no more, they now lie lifeless clay,
Let Tears be hushed: hope comes to soften grief,
The Trump shall sound & Lo they rise to life.

AIRLIE, ANGUS, PATRICK DAVIE WHO DIED 1760 AGED 11 YEARS

We of this child had great content,
For to get learning of God & Christ was his intent.
Tho' soon cut of the stage of time,
We dar not to refleck that we so soon did part,
For it was his Letter will,
That he God's counsel should fulfill.

The Faicheny stone was carved by James Faichney a mason, as his own family monument, possibly between 1700 and 1706. The top picture shows the parents at the top centre of the mural monument, with a second pair of portraits on the outside. Each figure has a poppy seed on top of the head signifying the sleep of death. The bottom picture shows the ten living children carved on either side of the main panel, the girls in long dresses and the boys in kilts. Their mother, Joanna Murray, was the first to die, and her portrait head with book was inserted with an inscription.

TWO EMINENT FIFERS

ST ANDREWS CATHEDRAL BURIAL GROUND, FIFE, ALLAN ROBERTSON, 1850

IN MEMORY OF ALLAN ROBERTSON
WHO DIED 1st SEPTEMBER 1850 AGED 44 YEARS.
HE WAS GREATLY ESTEEMED FOR
HIS PERSONAL WORTH AND FOR
MANY YEARS WAS DISTINGUISHED AS THE
CHAMPION GOLFER OF SCOTLAND.

ST ANDREWS CATHEDRAL BURIAL GROUND, FIFE, TOM MORRIS JUNIOR, 1875

IN MEMORY OF
TOMMY SON OF TOM MORRIS
WHO DIED 25th DECEMBER 1875 AGED 24 YEARS
DEEPLY REGRETTED BY NUMEROUS FRIENDS
AND ALL GOLFERS, HE TWICE IN SUCCESSION
WON THE CHAMPIONSHIP BELT
AND HELD IT WITHOUT RIVALRY.

Sixty golfing societies comtributed towards the erection of the monument. The tragic story is well known. Young Tom and his father were playing in a tournament at North Berwick. A telegram arrived to say that his wife had given birth to their first son and both were very ill. They crossed the Firth of Forth by boat, and landed at St Andrews to hear that mother and child were both dead. They say that Tommy never recovered; his death took place three months later. Beneath the mural (below) a flat stone commemorates the death of the famed 'Old Tom Morris'.

ST ANDREWS
CATHEDRAL BURIAL
GROUND, FIFE,
DETAILS FROM
THE OBELISK TO
ALLAN ROBERTSON,
1850

IN MEMORY OF
"TOMMY"
SON OF THOMAS MORRIS
WHO DIED 25TH DECEMBER 1875 AGED 24 YEARS

DEEPLY REGRETTED BY NUMEROUS FRIENDS AND ALL GOLFERS
HE THRICE IN SUCCESSION WON THE CHAMPION'S BELT
AND HELD IT WITHOUT RIVALRY AND YET WITHOUT ENVY
HIS MANY AMIABLE QUALITIES
BEING NO LESS ACKNOWLEDGED THAN HIS GOLFING ACHIEVEMENTS

THIS MONUMENT HAS BEEN ERECTED
BY CONTRIBUTIONS FROM SIXTY GOLFING SOCIETIES

ST ANDREWS
CATHEDRAL BURIAL
GROUND, FIFE,
TOMMY MORRIS,
1875

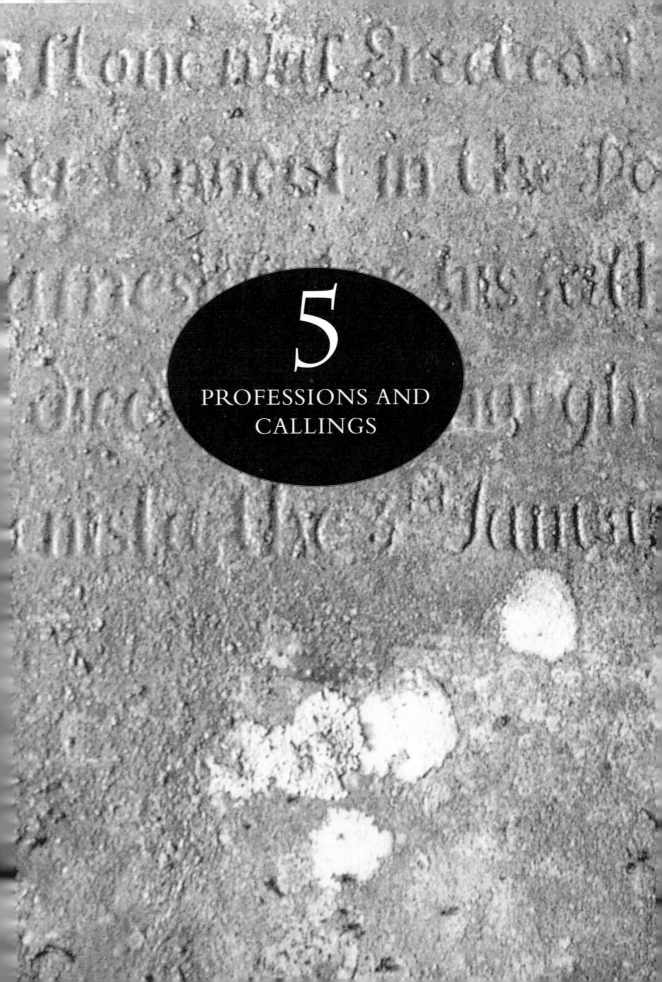

5

PROFESSIONS AND
CALLINGS

In 1567 the storm clouds gathered; James VI had always wanted to impose Episcopalianism on Scotland, but when he became King of England his wish to establish the English form of religion in Scotland became even stronger. He had the support of most of the Scottish nobles, but the majority of ministers were staunchly Presbyterian. James forbad the holding of General Assemblies; some ministers defied this by holding one in Aberdeen in 1605. As a result nineteen members were banished from Scotland. The most influential opponent to the King was Andrew Melville. James banished him to the continent for life.

There followed a series of acts which established Episcopacy, with the King himself having the sole right to appoint bishops. Over the years he forced a series of changes in the service, and in 1618 had the General Assembly pass 'The Five Articles of Perth', which went against Reformed doctrine and practice in regard to the Sacraments. This was to be the cause of the rebellion in the reign of Charles I, who succeeded to the throne in 1625 (although his coronation in Scotland did not take place until 1633). He had the same ideas as his father; in 1637 he announced that a new service book was to be introduced: 'The Book of Common Prayer' was to replace 'Knox's Liturgy', and had to be used by all ministers.

It was the torch to the conflagration; petitions were sent to the Privy Council from all parts of the country. The National Covenant was drawn up, a pledge to oppose all the recent changes in the form of worship. On the 28th February, 1638, in Greyfriars Church in Edinburgh, it was signed by a great body of noblemen and gentlemen, and copies were dispatched to all parts of the country. Eventually, because he needed the support of the Scots, the King agreed to what became known as the Westminster Treaty which settled Presbyterianism in Scotland. But the troubled times continued over the next decades, and came to a head in 1661, less than a year after the Restoration of Charles II to the throne, and Episcopacy was re-established. The sacrifices of the Covenanters were undone at one stroke.

The story of what was known as the 'Killing Time' is well known. James VII and II continued to maintain the claim of the Stewarts that they were appointed by God and were masters of the Church and State. The monuments to martyrs and to ministers of the Church record the strength of fellings, the sufferings, the fury against the establishment of Episcopacy. In this constant state of flux many ministers suffered great hardship, and were turned out of their manses, banished, imprisoned, and in some instances killed. In Wigtownshire, Ayrshire and Lanarkshire, and to a lesser extent in other parts of the Lowlands, there remain a great number of monuments to Covenanters. A Covenanters' Society is active in keeping these in good order.

With the crowning of William and Mary a new day dawned at last. In 1690 Presbyterianism was firmly and finally re-established. There were those who

PREVIOUS PAGE.
DETAIL. CORTACHY,
ANGUS,
JAMES WINTER,
1732

OPPOSITE.
PRESTWICK,
AYRSHIRE,
HUGH BO— &
JANET HUNTER,
1728.
THE PLOUGH SCENE
USUALLY APPEARS
AT THE BOTTOM OF
THE STONE AND
SHOWS THE
PLOUGHMAN, THE
GOADSMAN AND
THE TEAM OF OXEN,
SOMETIMES WITH
TWO HORSES

remained Episcopalian, and many of them joined in the Fifteen and Forty-five Rebellions in the hope that the Stewarts might restore their form of religion. But it was not until 1791 that the laws against Episcopalians were replaced, and in 1829 the Catholic Emancipation Act was passed. Accordingly one would not expect to find gravestones to dissenters in the parish churchyards. There were also disputes about the Patronage Act, and onwards from 1733 seceding churches were set up. The kinder religious philosophy of the Moderates and a warmer evangelicalism gradually replaced a God of Vengeance by a God of Love. Gradually the epitaphs lay less stress on sin and the grimmer doctrines of the Calvinists. Word and icon emphasised the hopeful side of death. In the eighteenth century, parish ministers were commemorated by mural tablets within the churches, and by mural monuments and tablestones in the kirkyards. In some cases the congregation contributed to the cost. The epitaphs dwell on the virtues of the minister and the length of service faithfully served; sometimes this was amazingly long as the minister held the tenure for life.

The minister and the schoolmaster were held in esteem, but of course there may have been others in the parish who attended university. From the time of the Reformation great stress had been laid on the value of education. After the 1696 Act attempts were increasingly made to establish a school in every parish, and to enable the 'lad o' pairts' who was gifted to move on to secondary and university education. But the financial difficulties or the reluctance of the heritors in many parishes made for poor provision of school buildings and schoolmasters' salaries. Yet in the eighteenth century, education of children in Scotland was more widespread than in many countries in Europe. The work of the schoolmaster was closely connected with the aims of the church: a recording by Rogers from a stone to a schoolmaster at Alloa begins:

> To guide the thoughts of youth to pious lore,
> To guard from ill and show the path of right,
> Their minds with solid principles to store
> He laboured much and laboured with delight.

Such was their poverty that many schoolmasters and their families lie in unmarked graves.

Both surgeons, who were relatively few in number, and physicians, who for a long time trained as apprentices, were much in demand by the minority who could afford to pay, yet their work was so often to no avail. 'Drogs and medicines did no good' states more than one epitaph. Families had to be philosophical about untimely losses; they were the result of original sin, as the popular rendering of the scene of the Fall of Man on many gravestones exemplified. God called when he saw fit. But there was good progress in the subjects of surgery and anatomy in the eighteenth century, when teachers at the Surgeons' Hall in Edinburgh attracted students who had previously had to travel to Holland. Glasgow University set up its School of Surgery in 1740.

In the graveyards are the remains of various measures to foil the Body Snatchers, such as iron mort-safes which enclosed the coffin, and mort-houses where the bodies were secured until decomposition made them of no use to the thieves. Elsewhere watch towers — small, windowed buildings — were erected near the churchyard entrances, and at night a rota of parishioners kept a watching vigil.

Many Scots soldiers died abroad; many perished in their own country in the turbulent times of the sixteenth and seventeenth centuries. Apart from the two rebellions, the eighteenth century was comparatively peaceful. But there are few monuments to Royalists who perished in their cause. However, shop-owners, ship-wrights, mariners and fishermen are commemorated in many graveyards by images and epitaphs.

PRELACIE AND PRESBYTERIE

HERE LIES ANDREW RICHMOND
who was killed by Bloody Graham of Claverhouse
June 1679 for his adherence to the Word of God
and For Christ's Reformation.

When bloody tyrants here did rage
Over the Lord's own heritage,
To persecute His noble cause
By Mischief framed into laws,
'Cause I the Gospel did defend,
By Martyrdom my life did end.

GLASSFORD OLD KIRK, LANARK, MR WILLIAM GORDON OF EARLSTON, 1679

To the Memory of the very worthy pillar of the
Church, Mr William Gordon of Earlston in Galloway,
shot by a party of Dragoons on his way to Bothwell
Bridge, 22nd June 1679, aged 65. Inscribed by his great
grandson Sir William Gordon Bart, 11th June 1772

Silent till now full ninety years hath stood
This humble monument of guiltless blood,
Tyrannic sway forbad his fate to name,
Least his known worth should prove the Tyrant's shame.
On Bothwell Road, with love of freedom fired,
The tyrants' minions boldly him required
To stop and yield, or it his life would cost;
On which they fired. Heaven so decreed his doom
Far from his own, laid silent in the tomb;
How leaug'u'd with patriots to maintain the cause.
Of true RELIGION, LIBERTY and LAWS.
How learn'd, how soft, his manner free from pride,
How clear his judgement, how he lived and died,
They well could tell who weeping round him stood,
On Steven's plains that drank his Patriot blood.

MEN OF THE CHURCH

DALKEITH, MIDLOTHIAN, MR JOHN VEITCH, MINISTER AT WESTRUTHER,
WHO DIED AT DALKEITH 1702, AGED 82

Old venerable Veitch his corps here lies,
His soul above, with Christ, in paradise;
Was sojourner and punisher of ill,
But of the truth a patrone ever still;
Upon God's work, himself he daily spent,
From what was others, great was his restraint.
Lo, after years twice fourty and near three,
A vi'lent fever clos'd thy works to thee;
Years fifty five thou taught thy dearest flock,
By word, by life, by prison and death's stroak.

MURAL MONUMENT, SORN, AYR, MR MUNGO LINDSAY, WHO DIED 1738

So long he lived in this same retreat,
Neather affecting to be known or great;
Humble & painful taught the great Concern
Which yet he thought he never enough could learn.
Skill in the sacred tongues of heavenly truth,
The only language of Jehova's mouth.
He led his flock through the delicious fields,
(Heaven's gentle dews & rains he yields);
Shuning lawsuits by deeds he us'd to write,
He sav'd their purse & cleared their rights;
& with rare bounty Gratified the Poor,
from the rich treasures of his blessed store;
& by the laws of God and man ascends
to his long dear & valuable friend.

KIRKOSWALD, AYR, MR PEEBLES, DIED 1676

HERE
MR PEEBLES
LEFT IN TRUST
HIS BODY TO BE TURNED TO DUST.
HIS FLOCK, HIS WIFE, HIS BAIRNS ELEVEN
REVIVES HIS NAME, HIMSELFS IN HEAVEN,
FOR PRAISED BE GOD, GRACE NEVER QUAT HIM,
IN LIFE NOR DEATH, TILL GLORY GAT HIM.
BORN 1594, ORDAINED 1617, ENTERED TRUST 1676

ST CUTHBERTS, EDINBURGH, THE REVD DAVID DICKSON, 1842

In Memory of
THE REVD DAVID DICKSON
who died 18th July 1842
This piece of sculture designed to represent an almost
daily occurrence in his life — has been erected
by a number of his parishioners
SCULPIT ALEX HANDYSIDE
(the minister is shown with orphaned children)

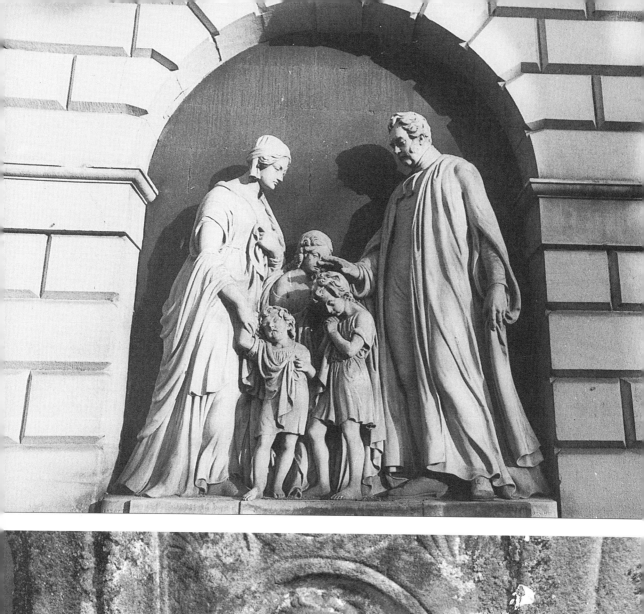

BARR, AYRSHIRE, THE REVEREND MR JOHN CAMPBELL 1743

HERE LYES THE CORPS OF
THE REVEREND MR. JOHN CAMPBELL
MINISTER OF THE GOSPEL 17 YEARS AT
BARR WHO DIED FEBRY.1743 AGED

SCHOOLMASTERS

MIGVIE, ABERDEEN, WILLIAM FLETCHER, SOMETIME MASTER
OF THE SOCIETY'S SCHOOL, WHO DIED 1769 AGED 48 YEARS

Enough, cold stone,
Suffice his long lov'd name;
Words are too weak
To pay his virtue's claim.
Temples and tombs,
And tongues shall waste away,
And power's vain pomp
In mouldering dust decay;
But ere mankind
A more laborious Teacher see,
Eternity, O Time, — shall bury thee.

AUCHTERMUCHTY, FIFE, FROM THE EPITAPH TO DAVID FERRY, 1726

In all the learning of the schools deep skill'd,
Which with a native modesty he veil'd.
Poor students found him generous and kind,
On his love-feasts they very often din'd,
He fed at once their body and their mind.
No miser, many of his goods did share,
Food to the needy gave, and cloth'd the bare.

OPPOSITE TOP.
ST CUTHBERT'S,
EDINBURGH,
THE REVD
DAVID DICKSON

OPPOSITE BELOW.
THE MINISTER
PREACHES FROM
THE PULPIT.
REVD MR JOHN
CAMPBELL, BARR,
AYRSHIRE, 1743

NEWTON, MIDLOTHIAN, THOMAS SOMMERVILLE, 1775

In memory of THOMAS SOMMERVILLE Schoolmaster
in this parish son to JOHN SOMMERVILLE FARMER
who died December 13th 1775 aged 37

PHYSICIANS AND MEN OF HEALING

GLASGOW HIGH KIRK, DOCTOR PEETER LOW, 1612

STAY PASSENGER AND VIOW THIS STONE,
FOR UNDER IT LYIS SUCH A ONE,
WHO CUIRED MANY WHILL HE LIEVED,
SOE GRACIOUS HE NOE MAN GREIVED,
YEA WHEN HIS PHYSICK'S FORCE OFT FAILED,
HIS PLESANT PURPOSE THEN PREVAILED;
FOR OF HIS GOD HE GOT THE GRACE,
TO LIVE IN MIRTH AND DIE IN PEACE.
HEAVIN HES HIS SOUL, — HIS CORPS THIS STONE,
SIGH PASSINGER AND SOE BE GONE.
AH ME! I GRAVELL AM AND DUST,
AND TO THE GRAVE DESHEND I MOST:
O PAINTED PIECE OF LIVEING CLAY,
MAN BE NOT PROUD OF THY SHORT DAY.

DALGARNOCK, DUMFRIESSHIRE, JOHN ADDISON, +1732

Here lieth the corps of
John Addison chirugeon
in Thornhill who died Decr
20th 1732 aged 42 years

The portrait of John Addison is balanced by a leafy caryatid with a foliate head
peeping from the bosom. With this, the soul, the bible and the flaming torch,
the medical man seems to be heading for Paradise.

ABOVE.
NEWTON
CHURCHYARD,
MIDLOTHIAN,
THOMAS
SOMMERVILLE,
SCHOOLMASTER,
DIED IN 1775

❖

BELOW.
DALGARNOCK,
DUMFRIESSHIRE,
JOHN ADDISON,
1732

ST CYRUS NETHER, JEAN STEVENSON AND THE WEBSTER CHILDREN, 1759

As runs the glass,
Man's life doth pass.
This monument was erected by Alexr Webster, tenant
in Ston of Morphie, and Bonesetter, in memory of his
wife and children. Patients queue to be treated by
the Bone Setter.

NEWTYLE, ANGUS, ROBERT MASON, TENANT, WHO DIED 1748 AGED 84 YEARS

ST CYRUS
NETHER
CHURCHYARD,
DETAIL OF THE
JEAN STEVENSON
& WEBSTER
CHILDREN STONE,
1759

Struck by the fiery dart of Death,
Here ROBERT MASON Lies,
Awaiting the Eternal Call
Of Christ beyond the Skies.
He while on earth mankind did aid,
& genarously befriend,
For which we hope, Almighty God,
has bless'd his latter end.
He by God's blessing often did,
Lame people Safe restore,
To wonted Strength, although their bones,
were bruised very sore.

SOLDIERS

FOULDEN, BERWICKSHIRE, GEORGE RAMSAY, DEPARTED 1592

FIFE. FOSTRING. PEACE. ME. BRED.
FROM. THENCE. THE. MERCE. ME. CALD.
THE. MERCE. TO. MARSIS. LAVIS. LED.
TO. BYDE. HIS. BATTELLIS. BOLD.
VERIED. VITH. VARES. AND. SORE. OPPREST.
DEATH. GAVE. TO. MARS. THE. FOYL.
AND. NOV. I. HAVE. MORE. QVYIET. REST.
THAN. IN. MY. NATIVE. SOYL.
FIFE. MERCE. MARS. MORT. THESE. FATAL. FOVR
ALL. HAIL. MY. DAYES. HES. DRIVEN. OVR.

AUCHTERHOUSE, ANGUS, JAMES STEUART, DIED 1730 AGED 62

In foreign lands where men with war engage,
He was sarvising at maney a bloody saige;
And was preserved unhurt, ye gathered to his rest
In good old age — who trusts in God is blist.

CORTACHY, ANGUS, JAMES WINTER, 1732

Here lyes James Vintner who died at Peathaugh
Who fought most valiantly at ye Water of Saugh
Along wit Ledenhendry, who did command ye day,
They vanquis the enemy & made them Runn away.

CORTACHY, ANGUS,
JAMES WINTER,
1732.
NOTE SWORD
AND BUCKLER
IN SHIELD. DETAIL,
SEE PAGE 75

THO BOREAS WAVE

WEST KILBRIDE, AYR, THOMAS RITCHIE, 1786

Though winds and waves and raging seas,
Have tost me to and fro,
Yet by the Hand of providence,
We harbour here below,
Safe from the dangers of them all,
And rest as in a sleep,
Till he who calleth us do call,
To join the vocal fleet.

FETTERCAIRN, ANGUS, ALEXANDER CROLL, 1751

He as a rock amongst vast Billows stood,
Scorning loud winds and raging of the flood;
And fix'd remaining all the force defies,
Muster'd from threat'ning seas, & thundering skies,
To keep amean his end still to observe,
And from the Laws of Nature neer to swerve.

MIDMAR, ABERDEEN, CHARLES MACKAY OF SHIELS, 1794

Both hot and cold, thro' every clime I've gone,
And felt the fierce extreme of either Zone;
Twice twenty times and eight the Atlantic cross'd;
With many Boisterous storms I have been toss'd.
Few of my fellow travellers lived to see
So many days as God has granted me:
Through all these storms and dangers I have past,
To this safe port I am arrived at last,
The wind may blow, the sea may rage and roar,
They never can disturb me any more.
(written by himself)

OPPOSITE LEFT.
BOTHKENNAR,
STIRLINGSHIRE,
ALEX AND MARGARET
SIMPSON,
1815.

OPPOSITE RIGHT.
DETAIL. COWIE,
KINCARDINSHIRE,
ALEX FALCONER,
1837

OLD KILPATRICK, DUMBARTON, WILLIAM DENNY, SHIPBUILDER

Genius and worth sleep in this honoured grave:
Here the quick brain — the active fingers lie,
But his mind's offspring proudly breast the wave
On every sea where Britains colours fly.

❖

KINNOUL, PERTHSHIRE, JOHN DUFF AND MARY MURRAY,
& JEAN THOMSON, 1782

. . . .
HERE LYES JEAN THOMSON SPOUSE TO
ALEX DUFF BOATMAN & BURGES
IN PERTH WHO DIED MAY 18th
1772 AGED 29 YEARS & THEIR
CHILDREN JEAN ALEX & PETER

This wonderful scene of the Ferryman on the Tay brings to mind the ancient
legend of the ferrying of the dead across the Styx. (Cover picture).

A MUSICIAN

GLAMIS, ANGUS, JAMES CHALMERS, MUSICIAN TO THE NOBLE
FAMILY OF STRATHMORE, WHO DYED 1770.

When minstrels from each place around,
To meetings did repair;
This man was still distinguished
By a refined air.
His powerful and his charming notes
So sweetly did constrain,
That to resist, and not to dance
Was labour all in vain.
He played with such dexterity,
By all it is confest,
That in this grave interred is
Of Violists the best.

THE STAGE

THE NECROPOLIS, GLASGOW, FROM THE EPITAPH TO
JOHN HENRY ALEXANDER OF THE THEATRE ROYAL,
GLASGOW, WHO DIED 1851

Fallen is the curtain. the last scene is o'er,
The favourite actor treads life's stage no more.
Oft lavish plaudits from the crowd he drew,
And laughing eyes confessed his humour true,
Here fond affection rears its sculptured stone
For virtues not enacted, but his own

COUPAR ANGUS, PERTH, MR THOMAS BELL, COMEDIEN,
LATE OF THE THEATRE ROYAL EDINBURGH 1815

'A respectable performer, an agreable companion, and an
honest man. While on the <u>Stage</u> of Life he encountered some
of the rudest shocks of adversity, and felt the chill grip of
penury in many a checquered <u>Scene</u>; but, possessed of a happy
equanimity of temper, a social disposition, and a well
informed mind, the arrows of misfortune fell powerless. On

the 31st of August, 1815, the <u>Curtain</u> of fate dropt on his <u>Drama</u> of his existence, and he <u>Retired</u> from the <u>Theatre</u> of the world, to the sorrow and regret of all those who had the pleasure of his acquaintance.

A POET

THE CANONGATE CHURCHYARD, EDINBURGH, ROBERT FERGUSSON, 1774

No sculptur'd Marble here, nor pompous lay,
No storied Urn, nor animated Bust;
This simple stone directs pale SCOTIA's way,
To pour her sorrows o'er the Poet's dust.

A CHAMBERLAIN

BIGGAR, PEEBLES, FROM THE EPITAPH TO
MR. ALEXANDER WARDLAW, CHAMBERLAIN TO
THE EARL OF WIGTON, DIED 1721

Here lies a man, whose upright heart
With virtue was profusely stor'd,
Who acted well the honest part
Between the tenants and their lord.
Between the sands and flinty rock
Thus steer'd he in the golden mean,
While his blyth countenance bespoke
A mind unruffled and serene.

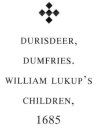

DURISDEER,
DUMFRIES.
WILLIAM LUKUP'S
CHILDREN,
1685

SOUTH
LEITH
CHURCHYARD,
EDINBURGH,
THE CARTER'S
STONE,
N.D

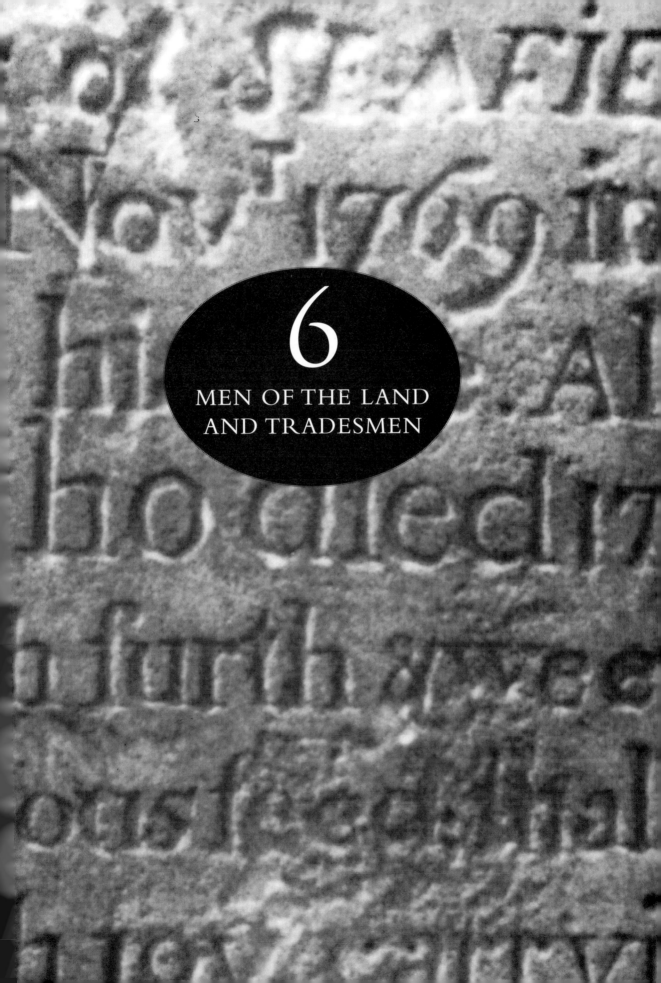

6

MEN OF THE LAND
AND TRADESMEN

The tombs of landed gentry are often in private burial grounds, or within the churches, or in the churchyards in aisles or in the form of prestigious mural monuments. They may be classical and comparitively simple, or they may have stone or marble effigies.

Tenant farmers denoted their rank by describing themselves in this way in the epitaph, or occasionally by use of the word 'in' before the name of the farm, in contrast to the word 'of' which would denote ownership. The picture opposite, is in the churchyard at Temple, Midlothian and is fine portrait of John Craig of Outorstoun with two litle boys. In the eighteenth century when innovative men brought in new and more productive methods of farming, an increased income enabled tenant farmers to erect handsome tombs. In the Lothians, especially in East Lothian, there are many elaborate tablestones and mural monuments which are heavily adorned with classical features and skilfully carved emblems. The scene of the Sower and the Harvester is the favourite there, and relates to the quotation from the Scriptures 'What man sowing precious seed and going forth doth mourn?' There was good farming land in Angus and parts of Perthshire, and the custom was to select a fine headstone with a wide range of emblems, a shield with profuse mantling, and a display of sock and coulter to stand for the plough. Sometimes a whole plough was chosen, as at Carmylie, with the words writ large proclaiming 'WE PLOW IN HOPE'. In Ayrshire the carvings are usually cruder and the plough scene was favoured. (see previous page).

One might suppose that the foliate head would be chosen by farmers and by gardeners, but its popularity stems more from regional fashions. East Lothian abounds in the emblem, but so do tombs to farmers — and also it was chosen by many professional and tradesmen. In Angus and East Perthshire many tenant farmers commissioned the masons to carve biblical scenes of Adam and Eve or of Abraham and Isaac, or of the Resurrection, and in addition a rhyming epitaph, with no need to stint the number of words. Of course there were others who had the money for such monuments, and poor folk who made sacrifices in order to mark the graves of their loved ones and bolster their hopes of a reunion in Heaven. The widow of a miller at Strichen, Aberdeenshire, carried for some miles a grinding stone on which she had an epitaph cut. This was indeed an expression of devotion.

In the cities and the burghs the Trade Incorporations assumed great importance. The merchants who had been all powerful lost their dominance and the composition of the Town Councils became more democratic. By the eighteeenth century monuments indicate that there were still prosperous merchants, but also in the Merchant Guildry many keepers of small shops. Their emblem was the sign which looks like a figure 4, but was not intended to be such, and in fact was sometimes a reversed 4 sign. It appeared on bales of merchandise as early as the twelth century, and is thought to have been an

PREVIOUS PAGE.
DETAIL.
THOMAS GRAHAM,
FARMER, DIED AGED
61, INTERRED WITH
7 OF HIS CHILDREN.
1769

OPPOSITE.
TEMPLE
CHURCHYARD,
MIDLOTHIAN,
JOHN CRAIG OF
OUTORSTOUN,
+1742

adaptation of the chi rho sign; this was from the first two letters of the name of Christ in Greek. It was adopted into the arms of the Stirling Merchant Guildry, and from thence appeared on tombstones in a wide band across central Scotland, one of the earliest being on a 1582 monument at the Howff, Dundee.

The pride men experienced in their trade and skills is proclaimed in the graveyards of cities and rural parishes. The tools of trade which embellished the banners and mort-cloths of the Incorporations were carved on the gravestones, often within shields. The rhyming epitaphs beloved by them extolled their skills, their virtues and their religious beliefs. The graveyard presents a stone museum and a witness to the immensity of the changes which took place from century to century.

The headstones of members of the trades at Greyfriars Burial Ground at Perth, and at The Howff Dundee, evoke the centuries when Incorporations acted as both welfare and disciplinary bodies and were the core of social status. In a country parish churchyard you may find testimonies to the strata of society: Lairds, Ministers, Schoolmasters, farmers, smiths, weavers, tailors, shoemakers, millers, and gardeners. There are others, according to the locality, such as mariners by the coast, salmon fishers up the rivers, glovers and goldsmiths and lawyers in the cities. But rarely will you find a monument to a labourer, a miner, or a worker at the saltpans.

HUSBANDRIE

BRECHIN, ANGUS, ST MAGDALEN'S CHAPEL, JOHN ROB, 1740

Of all the Imployments that may be found
Husbandrie ought to be crowned.

GLAMIS, ANGUS, FROM THE EPITAPH TO DAVID KID, 1697

DEAR PILGRIMS, READ THIS ELEGY,
AND SPIRITUALIZ MORTALITY:
VICE I DECLIN'D, MY LYFE WAS JUST,
IN TILLAGE I BETRAYED NOT TRUST.
DAVID BY NAME, SURNAMED KID;
KIND TO THE POOR, NOW DIGNIFIED
IN BLISSED STATE, TRIUMPHANT HY,
DEATH'S STING PLVCK'T OUT,
SIN'S SOURSE IS DRY.
READ GRAVELY, PILGRIM, MIND THY DOOME
GOD RAPS ME UP FROM ILL TO COME.

LIVINGSTON, WEST LOTHIAN, THOMAS GRAHAM, +1769

He that goeth forth & weepeth
bearing precious seed shall doubt
less return with joy, carrying his
sheaves

AUCHTERMUCHTY, FIFE, ANDREW RICHARDSON, 1730

Beneath this Burial Stone a Tenant lys.
Andrew Richardson in Ridie Leys
Who died on the seventh in May & 1730.
A husbandman who ploughed in art
In hope he sowed and in reap did partake.
With skill the produce of the earth improved,
And to his wife and children whom he loved
With judgement he bequeathed his honest gain

The picture at the top of the next page shows two naked Resurrection figures
flanking an inverted crown a trumpet and the open bible inscribed 'I am that I am'.

THOMAS GRAHAM,
FARMER, DIED AGED 61,
INTERRED WITH 7
OF HIS CHILDREN.
1769. SEE DETAIL ON
PAGE 93

THE MERCHANTS

READER, WHO ON THIS STONE DOES
CAST THINE EYE,
DO NOT FORGET THE BLESSED MEMORY
OF BAILLIE JAMES CARSTAIRS; TO
WHOM GOD DID IMPART
A CANDIDE MIND, WITHOUT A DOUBLE HEART.
TO VIRTUE, GRACE AND HONESTY INCLIN'D;
TO ALL HIS FRIENDS MOST SINGULARLY KIND;
HE WISELY DID, WITH ALL MEN, FOLLOW PEACE;
AT LENGTH EXPYR'D FULL BOTH OF
YEARS AND GRACE.

THIS STONE IS ERECTED BY
ELIZTH STIRLING IN MEMORY
OF JOHN MORGAN HER DE

CEASED HUSBAND LATE
MERCHANT IN DUNDEE & TENN
ANT IN BALLHILL WHO DIED
YE 8 THE NOVR 1756 AGED 49
YEARS INTERRD WITHIN
Aequo pede sat Pauperum odernas reges

In this symbolic scene, shown in picture above, the merchant stands at his counter and writes in his book. A tiny hand holds the scales and is repeated alternately round the inner border. The alternate diamonds hold flaming hearts, an unusual emblem which this mason carved on most of the stones he cut. The sock and coulter of the plough indicate that he had some land.

BY HAMMER AND HAND ALL ARTS DO STAND

GREYFRIARS BURIAL GROUND, PERTH PATRICK GOW, 1693

Til God hath wrought us to his will
The hammer we shal suffer still
HERE LYE PATRICK GOU Hammerman
and late Convener in Perth
The hand of God comes from the clouds, and
He wraps on the anvil.

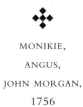

MONIKIE,

ANGUS,

JOHN MORGAN,

1756

100

EPITAPHS
AND IMAGES
FROM
SCOTTISH
GRAVEYARDS

Here Lyes PATRICK GOW, Hammerman
Who Departed This Life The 26TH Year
Of His Age.

LARGS, AYR, THEOPHILUS RANKIN, 1724

Of all mechanicks we have renown,
Above the hammer we wear the crown.

MONIKIE, ANGUS, JOHN RITCHIE, 1762

A most expert artificer in iron and brass
This stone was Erected by
Janet Blair in Memory of her
Deceased Husband John Ritchie
Late Smith in Lonhead of Auckenlake
Who died February 24 1760 Aged
50 years
Blist with Nin Children

INVERKEILOR, ANGUS, JAMES BURNESS, BLACKSMITH, 1847

My sledge and hammer lie declined;
My bellows now have lost their wind,
My fire's extinct, my forge decayed,
And in the dust my vice is laid.
My fire is spent, my iron gone,
My nails are drove, my day is done;
My fire-dried corps lies here at rest;
My soul like smoke soars to be blest.

KINNELL, ANGUS, JOHN URQUHART, 1731

If you would know who lies beneath this stone
A mechanic, Faber Lignarius, he was one
Who in his day for science was exceling
Yet with the worms he's taken up his dwelling
For neither airt though fine, nor skill ere can
Exime us from the common lot of man.

DETAIL.
MONIKIE, ANGUS,
THE GIBSON CHILDREN,
1765. SHOWING
THE SMITH AND HIS
APPRENTICE
AT THE ANVIL

102

EPITAPHS
AND IMAGES
FROM
SCOTTISH
GRAVEYARDS

A WATCHMAKER

INVERARITY, ANGUS, MARGARET RAMSAY, SISTER TO DAVID RAMSAY, 1772

The good thou hast a mind to do
Let it be quickly done
We every day expect to see
How soon the glass is run

THE GARDENERS

KINNELL, ANGUS, JOHN HALL, 1720

Any man who please to speir
JOHN HALL lyes here;
Nothing in life did betid him,
But honest men may lye bside him.
Sometime in Gardnerie he serv'd.
And from the truth he never swervd:

THE TOOLS
OF A WATCHMAKER
WHO ERECTED
THIS MONUMENT
TO HIS SISTER
ARE PERFECTLY
CARVED IN THE
SMALL SHIELD

He to his master ay was just,
& never did betray his trust:
& with his work did well Agree,
He father was of many A tree.
Att Knock-Millie-hill where he did dwell,
His produk their it Looketh well,
Now when he is dead its to be known;
Likewayes one his Children shown
With Spaid & Raik he Wrought his life,
With snading ax and pruning knife.
All these he wrought but any thraw,
With shouel fin and cutting saw,
The truth of All if you will ken,
He still was loved of honest men
That is in health today.

THE WEAVERS

FARNELL, ANGUS, JOHN DEAR, 1729

My days are swifter than a weaver's shuttle
The weaver's art it is renowned so
That Rich nor Poor without it could not go
To learn God's holy laws.

AUCHTERHOUSE, ANGUS, PATRICK MILLER, 1733

What is man's life that Swifter far
Than weaver's shuttle flies,
So troubles born he weeps a while
And mourns, sighs, groans, then dies.
Pray then improve the shining hour
Repent, do not delay
For who can promise on the next
That is in health today

The picture at the top right of the opposite page shows the reed of the loom, the stretchers and the shuttle.

In Carnie sure did DAVID die,
We hope his soul's in Heaven high;
The body lies beneath this stone,
To moulder there both skin and bone.
It was his blessed will to wear
A coat without a seam,
Which fitted well in every part,
Wove in a wyver's leem.

THE SHOEMAKERS

There are a good number of headstones with carvings of the crown, which the shoemakers assumed as wielders of the hammer, with the cordiner's knife, the awl, pliers, and the lasts which show the changing fashions in shoes. Each trade vied to proclaim its importance through a link wih the Bible. At Crail the Shoemakers' loft had the words 'How beautiful are thy feet with shoes'! (see opposite, below right).

THE TAILORS

GLAMIS, ANGUS, WILLIAM CRUIKSHANK, 1731

Rare William who will not thy name
And memory still love;
Since you the trade did all around
So wondrously did improve.
Our Tradesmen justly did to thee
Pre-eminence allow,
Being taught the rudiments of Art
Or else refin'd by you.
That skill of yours did on them all
An ornament reflect;
And as you liv'd so did you die,
In honour with respect.

TOP LEFT.
ST FILLANS,
FORGAN, FIFE,
JOHN CHRISTIE,
1841.
THESE ARE THE
USUAL TOOLS
CARVED ON A
GARDENER'S STONE,
BUT THE WATERING
CAN IS A RARE
EMBLEM.

BELOW LEFT.
MONIKIE CHURCHYARD,
ANGUS, DETAIL
OF STONE TO THE
GIBSON CHILDREN,
1759

106

❖

EPITAPHS
AND IMAGES
FROM
SCOTTISH
GRAVEYARDS

ST FILLANS, FORGAN, MARGARET DAVIDSON, 1705

HERE.LYES
MARGARET.DAVIDSON
SPOUSE.TO.JAMES
KILPATRICK.WHO
DEPARTED.1701
AND.OF.HER.AGE

ST FILLAN,

FORGAN, FIFE,

MARGARET DAVIDSON,

1705

This folk art carving makes a strong impact; the tailor's shears, flat iron and bodkin are topped by what may be a thimble — or is it a crown?

THE MILLERS

The millers were not on the whole popular: the tenant farmer was bound to take his corn to the mill to which his land was thirled. Accordingly there was no competition, no free enterprise, and millers were accused of taking more than was their due. The farmers were responsible for keeping the mills and mill leads in good order. The number of mills on some small rivers was amazing; besides corn mills for threshing corn, there were also flour mills, spinnning mills, fulling mills, and saw mills. The main emblem of the miller is the mill rind, the iron part of which supports the upper part of the mill wheel, and carries the eye which rests upon the end of the spindle.

CAMPSIE, DUNBARTONSHIRE, TO AN UNKNOWN MILLER:

Eternity is
A wheel that turns
A wheel that turned ever,
A wheel that turns
And will leave turning never

THE MALTMEN AND BREWERS

DALMENY, WEST LOTHIAN, AGNES MURE, 1722

The picture above shows the 'Stingmen' who carried the casks of ale to the customers. They were known as 'Sting and Ling'. Each has a jug; the clay bung seems to be out of the cask. Their usual emblems on monuments are the sheaf of corn, the longhandled brewer's brush, the shovel with wooden slats and the firehook. We have yet to find a rhyming epitaph on a stone to maltman or brewer.

THE FLESHERS

ST ANDREWS CATHEDRAL MUSUEM, FIFE, JOHN VENNISON, 1654

❖

DALMENY
CHURCHYARD,
AGNES MUIR,
+1722

Here lyes a godly and industrious young man
John Vennison, noted for his high reputation
and his uprightness, a citizen of this city
and once Deacon of the Fleshers Incorporation
who died on 7 of August AD 1654 the thirty
second of his age

This monument is one of a collection of grand coped stones which were erected in the Cathedral grounds in the seventeenth century. Most of the inscriptions are in Latin. Here we see the one-time Deacon in his death bed, his bible in his hand and dog at his side. The King of Terrors attacks with death's dart. The tools in the shield are axe, cleaver, and sharpener.

THE MASONS

In only a few instances we have been referring to the work of masons who may have carved tombstones at some distance from their centre. Those who cut most of the eighteenth century headstones were local men who worked on the erection and repair of buildings. Unlike the medieval travelling schools of masons, who inscribed mason marks to indicate their part of the team work in the whole fabric, the later local masons gave no clues as to htheir identity. There was no need; everyone would know who had cut each newly set-up monument. It is possible to discover and list the work of an eighteenth century mason by the style of his carvings and lettering. Sometimes, as in the case of the Hart stone (pl. 21), we find a name. These masons worked in a limited

ST ANDREWS,
CATHEDRAL MUSEUM,
JOHN VENNISON,
1654

110

EPITAPHS
AND IMAGES
FROM
SCOTTISH
GRAVEYARDS

locality; the best-known of them may have had commisssions to cut stones for up to six adjoining parish churchyards.

POLMONT, STIRLINGSHIRE,
THE HART CHILDREN, 1766

HERE lyes Christian Hart daughter to Robert Hart Mason in Reading she died May 8 1745 aged 2 years. Also Mary Heart died October 19th 1752 aged 3 years — months. Also Janet Heart died September 2 1760 aged 2 years 2 months. Also Helen Hart died July 26th 1766 aged 11 years.

POLMONT,
STIRLINGSHIRE,
THE HART CHILDREN,
1766.
THE FATHER OF
THESE CHILDREN
WAS A MASON AND
MAY HAVE CARVED
THIS STONE. THE
THREE CASTLES
IN A SHIELD ARE
THE MASON'S
EMBLEM

THE WRIGHTS

DUNNICHEN, ANGUS,
ROBERT PULLAR, 1782

In memory of Robert Pullar
who died agust 20 in the
22 year of his age
This young man died before his prime,
God called him hence when he tho't time.

It is unusual to find three souls; the elaborate border designs are typical of this mason. (See page 46).

THE CARTERS

THE CARTERS' STONE, SOUTH LEITH CHURCHYARD, EDINBURGH

Great God whose potent arm drives the sun,
The Carters bless while wheels of time shall run
Of old they drove thy sacred arc, O God
Guide thou their Hands and Steps in every road.
Protect this horse we dedicate to thee,
Increase and sanctify our sanctity.

This stone built into the wall shows the area belonging to this trade. Unusually, the Incorporations in this parish had burial lairs in the churchyard corresponding in position to the galleries they held inside the church. (See page 92).

112

EPITAPHS
AND IMAGES
FROM
SCOTTISH
GRAVEYARDS

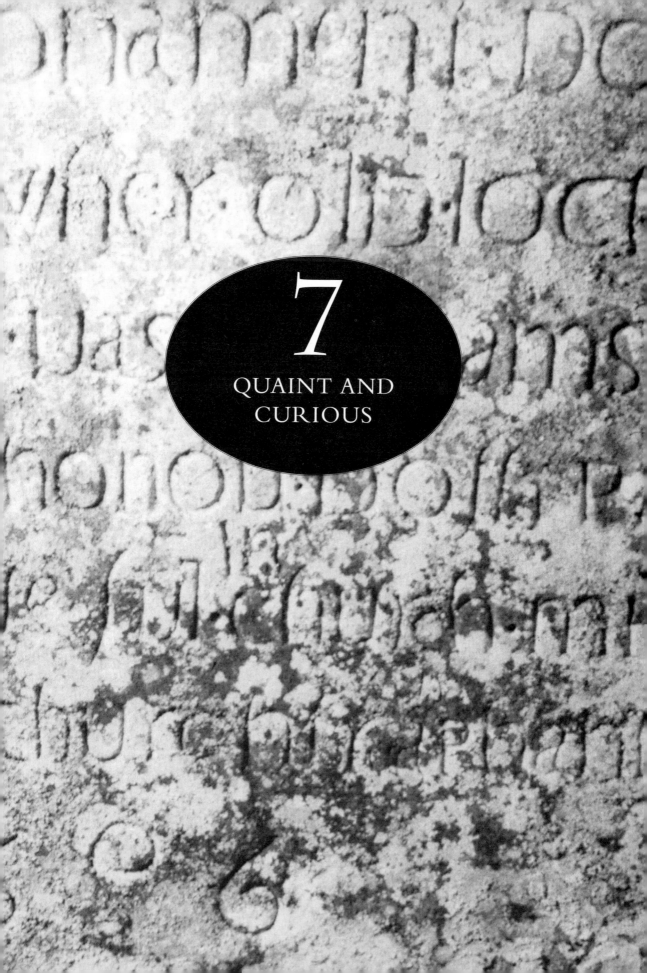

7

QUAINT AND CURIOUS

AH! JOHN WHAT CHANGES SINCE I SAW THEE LAST,
THY FISHING AND THY SHOOTING DAYS ARE PAST,
BAGPIPES AND HAUTBOYS THOU CANST SOUND NO MORE,
THY NODS, GRIMACES, WINKS AND PRANKS ARE O'ER.
THY HARMLESS QUEERISH INCOHERENT TALK,
THY WILD VIVACITY AND TRUDGING WALK
WILL SOON BE QUITE FORGOT; THY JOYS ON EARTH
A SNUFF, A GLASS, RIDDLES AND NOISY MIRTH
ARE VANISH'D ALL. YET BLEST I HOPE THOU ART
FOR IN THY STATION WEEL THOU PLAYD'ST THY PART

Most collections contain examples of humourous and quaint epitaphs. In Scotland, and to a lesser extent in England, the majority of these were handed down by word of mouth, or appeared in print, either in books, in broadsheets or newspapers. Many of them are derogatory about the dead, or even lewd. It is unlikely that they were ever cut on churchyard monuments. An example from England is the following, said to be on the tomb of Sir Nathaniel Wraxall the historian, who died in 1831:

> Men, measures, scenes, and facts all
> Misquoting, misstating,
> Misplacing, misdating,—
> Here lies Sir Nathaniel Wraxall

It is hard to conceive that the Church of Scotland would approve of such levity. But one never knows! Was there ever a stone at Crail which reputedly bore the following?

> Here lies my good and gracious Auntie
> Whom Death has packed in his portmanty,
> Three score and ten years God did gift her,
> And here she lies, wha' de'il daurs lift her?

One relishes such a surprising epitaph; there was, and is, a universal need to cock a snook at Grim Death; to alleviate the grief with a smile; and in the face of the many eulogies which proclaim an almost unreal perfection of character, to insert a malicious human foible. Read those somewhat scurrilous epitaphs in a collection of the poems of Robert Burns; they must have been well received, but they appeared in print and were not cut in stone. One of the mildest is to Gabriel Richardson:

> Here brewer Gabriel's fire's extinct,
> And empty are his barrells;
> He's blest, if as he brewed he drink,
> This man of honest morals!

In the minutes of the Brechin Kirk Session for 1619 is the following entry: 'The Session considering the monie abuses are admittat in making epitaphs by young men in this citie affixing on burial stanes anything they ples, partlie rediculous and partlie ontrew, ordain that no epitaph shall be put on any monuments without the approval of the Session'. This may be one origin of the many amusing and defamatory epitaphs published in various collections. It may explain, for instance, the conflict of two claims for an epitaph on a gravestone at the Howff, Dundee. The actual epitaph reads:

OPPOSITE.
IN 1777 THERE
WAS A COMPETITION
FOR THE BEST
COMPOSITION TO
COMMEMORATE
JOHN MURRAY
A POPULAR
GAMEKEEPER
AT KELLS,
KIRKCUDBRIGHT.
THE MINISTER
WON THE PRIZE.

116

❖

EPITAPHS
AND IMAGES
FROM
SCOTTISH
GRAVEYARDS

HEAR LYES ANE HONEST ANE GODLY MAN, JOHNE ROCHE BRABENER AND BVRGES OF DVNDIE QHVA DEPARTIT THIS LYFE THE 10 OF FEBRVAR 1616 ZEIRIS BEING OF AGE 43 ZEIRIS WITH HIS SPOVSE EVPHIANE PYE QHVA HES CAVSIT THIS TO BE MADE IN REMEMBRANCE OF HIM AND THEIR 14 BEARNES.

The one which is often reported to be on the tombstone runs:

Here I lie, Epity Pye,
My twenty bairns, my guidman and I'

My favourite one comes from an American book of Comic Epitaphs, but so far I have not had the opportunity of establishing whether the stone is really to be found in a cemetery at Harwich Port.

SACRED TO THE REMAINS OF
JONATHAN THOMPSON
A PIOUS CHRISTIAN AND
AFFECTIONATE HUSBAND;
HIS DISCONSOLATE WIDOW
CONTINUES TO CARRY ON
HIS GROCERY BUSINESS
AT THE OLD STAND ON
MAIN STREET CHEAPEST
AND BEST PRICES IN TOWN

Essentially epitaphs are epigrammatic and neat, and as such they are sometimes witty. It is often written that the tomb of David Hume the philosopher, so prominent on the Calton Hill, Edinburgh, bears the splendidly neat epigram:

Within this circular Idea
Called vulgarly a Tomb
The Ideas and Impressions lie
That constituted Hume.

However, Monteith reported that the only inscription was 'David Hume Esq. Born 16th April 1711, died 26th August 1776' — which seems regrettable.

The Faber Book of Epigrams and Epitaphs introduced and selected by Geoffrey Grigson, suggests that not only *The Greek Collection* but equally Martian's epigrams were sources for many writers of the 16th to the 19th centuries. He writes 'They have pleased themselves [and their readers] with being gnomic and witty and delicate and brutal and grotesque. They have written for fun, decently and indecently'. This seems to me to give a clue as to the influence of the epigram on the epitaph. Many such are quoted by Pettigrew, for instance, for Sir Henry Wooten (1536-1639):

> He first deceased, she for a little tried
> To live without him, liked it not, and died.

From Scottish graveyards are the following succinct lines:

> Cupar Fife, William Rymar, Maltman, 16 —
> THROUGH CHRIST I AM NOT INFERIOR
> TO WILLIAM THE CONQUEROR

Clackmannan Churchyard, — 1761:

> I AM LAID IN THIS COLD BED
> AND MY COVERING OVER ME IS LAID

At St Andrews Cathedral Burial Ground, Fife, there is an obelisk to Captain Lumsdaine, his wife and children, possibly erected in 1858, with the inscription:

> Here we lie in a horizontal position
> Like a ship laid up and stripped
> of her sail and rigging.

A minister who had been invited to transfer to Mouswald from Kirkpatrick Juxta died before he took up office. Rogers gives the lines on his tombstone as:

> The Rev. Dr Stewart's call to Mouswald
> Was turned into a call to another land

The grim message of an epitaph is often softened by a quaintness of ideas, of spelling, of phrases. These epitaphs are not of our time, even though the message may be a universal one. A stone from Carsphairn, Kirkcudbrightshire, has some interesting features: study the photograph first (on page 112). Is this what was intended?

> this monyment DOO nou tell
> where old lockhead intereD vas
> his nams DarKinmay vho nou DOth prais
> and not patnise sin and mili(t)ating
> And in the church triumphant.

Consider the charm and the appeal of the epitaph to John Budworth of Glamis, Angus, who died in 1718:

118

❖

EPITAPHS
AND IMAGES
FROM
SCOTTISH
GRAVEYARDS

Here lyes JOHN BUDWORTH, English born,
Whose life these virtues did adorn —
He was both curteous, kynd & just,
A friend whom on might firmly trust;
Tho' lodged but in a crazy shrine,
Death smott the pott, thus sadly rent
And here to ly, the shell has sent.

And from Meigle, Perth, Jean Smith, aged 27, 1775:

If drogs or meedson
or ought from death could save
Shour this woman had not gon
So shoon into hir grave.

This stone was erected at Kinnoul, Perth, by Anne Irvine:

"in memory of her husband Andrew Sharp, cobbler, musician
and drawing master, and affectionate husband, a faithful friend
and an honest man. He died 5th Feby 1817 aged 37 years.
Halt for a moment, passenger and read,
Here Andrew dozes in his daisied bed,
Silent his flute, and torn off the key,
His pencils scattered and his muse set free."

There was a devout belief in a simple and fundamentalist view of death, and some
expresssions of this may now seem curious. This is shown in an epitaph at Edzell,
Angus, on a panel, a remnant from a tablestone, and refers to the Resurrection:

But yet the weight of flesh and blood,
doe soe her flight restraine,
That oft I prease, but doth small good,
I rise and fall again.

With the same notion is the following at Strathmartine, Angus, on a
monument to John Hall and his loving young wife Cathren Ramsay:

BOTH IN ONE GRAVE VNTIL THE TYM ACORD
THAT THEY SHALL HEIR THE EARCH ANGEL OF THE LORD;
OVR SOUL DOTH BEND OVR BODES STRAIGHT AND EVEN,
AS WITH IT SELFE IT WOLD THEME RAISE TO HEAVEN;
BVT ALL IN VAINE IT VNDERGOES SVCH TOYLE,

THE BODY WILL NOT LEVE ITS NATIVE SOYLE.
AGE PVLS IT DOWNE, AND MAKES IT STOOPE FVLL LOW,
TILL DEATH DOTH GIVE HIS FATALL OVERTHROW:
THEN THROVGH THE BODIES BREACH THE SOVL DOTH RIS,
AND LIKE A CONQVEROR MOVNT THE SKIES,
TO ITS ETERNAL REST FROM WHENCE IT CAME,
AS IS THER BODIES IN TOMS HERE LYES

The epitaph at Kilmarnock to Thomas Samson, 1795, runs:

Tam Samson's weel worn clay here lies,
Ye canting zealots spare him;
If honest worth in heaven arise,
Ye'll mend or ye win near him.

At Kilbirnie, James Orr, weaver, erected a stone (now lost) to his wife Agnes
Allan, who died in 1775. On one side of the stone, under a Trepresentation of
a herald, a sluggard and Death, and based on Proverbs VI v.6 and Rev. XX11
v.12, are the following quaint lines:

Awake thou sluggard of the dust,
The eternal son doth cry,
Forth into judgement come thou must
Thy actions for to try.
O all ye saints who's full of wants
Love God and sin abhor,
From sin I rest and every blast,
In this my silent bower.

Recorded as having once been on a stone at Haddington, East Lothian are
some lines which reveal that the classics were read, but not taken too seriously:

Hout Atropos hard-hearted Hag,
To cut the sheugh of Jamie Craig;
For had he lived a wheen mae years
He had been owre teugh for your sheirs;
Now Jamie's deid, sua maun we a',
And for his sake I'll say this sa
IN Hei'en Jamie, be thy saul.

120

❖

EPITAPHS
AND IMAGES
FROM
SCOTTISH
GRAVEYARDS

At Pittenweem, Fife, on the headstone to the wife of John Brown a watchmaker, are inscribed the words from Hebrews 1.v.12:

'Be ye not sluggish but imitators of those
who through patience inherit the promises.'

Anagrams and puns may occasionally be found; here is an early one, on the entry to the 1560 vault to the family of Porterfield, at Kilmacolm:

BVREIT HEIR LYIS
THAT DEATH DEFYIS
OF PORTERFIELDS THE RACE;
ARE HEIRS OF GLOIR THROU GRACE
THIS ANAGRAME VNFOLD MY BVILDAR SAL,
HIS NAME QVHA VIL UNTO THIS SENTENCE SEIK;
TIL FLIE THE IL: MAK GVID REPORT OF AL:
GVILLIAME SAL FIND, PORTERFIELD OF THAT ILK.
ZEIRS SEVINTIE FYVE, TO LIVE, HE LIVIT AND MO:
AND NOV FOR AY LIVS WITH THE GODS BVT SO.

The name which gives the unique identity of a person, at birth, at marriage, at death, is an integral part of the epitaph and is often woven into the verses, as at Errol, Perthshire, on the tomb of the Revd Mr Bell who died in 1665.

HERE CEAST AND SILENT LIES SWEET SOUNDING BELL,
WHO UNTO SLEEPING SOULS RUNG MANY A KNELL;
DEATH CRACKT THIS BELL, YET DOTH HIS PLEASANT CHIMING
REMAIN WITH THOSE WHO ARE THEIR LAMPS A-TRIMMING.
IN SPITE OF DEATH HIS WORD SOME PRAISE STILL SOUNDS
IN CHRIST'S CHURCH, AND IN HEAVEN HIS JOY ABOUNDS.

In the seventeenth century poems were composed so that the first word of each line, read vertically, gave the name of the deceased. Another type punned on the name: for instance on the tomb of Christiane Brydie at St Andrews Cathedral Museum are the words:

THOUGH IN THIS
TOMBE MY BONES
DO ROTTING LYE
YET READ MY NAME
FOR CHRIST ANE
BRYDE AM I. 1656

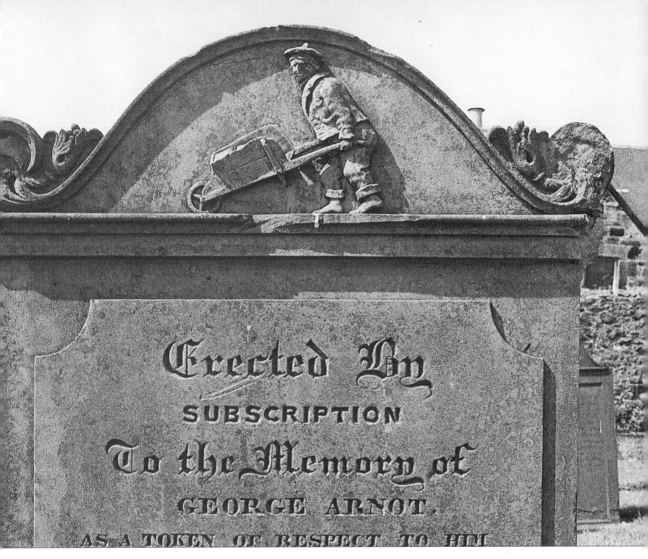

What seems to me most intriguing are those epitaphs which describe unusual characters, such as John Murray's, the gamekeeper at Kells (see page 114). It is my favourite epitaph, although that of George Arnot, below, is particularly poignant. It is only through epitaphs that we have so many glimpses into the characters and lives of so-called 'ordinary' people who lived long ago.

Erected by Subscribers
To the Memory of George Arnot
as a token of respect to him
for his usefulness to the public
he died there 27th March 1850 aged 35 years

His mind was weak, his body strong,
His answer ready with a song,
A mem'ry like him few could boast
Yet suddenly his life he lost.

BURNTISLAND,

FIFE,

GEORGE ARNOT,

1850

INDEX TO PLACE NAMES

BIBLIOGRAPHY

Andrews, William, *Curious Epitaphs*, Hull 1883

Bakewell, Joan and Drummond, John, *A Fine and Private Place*, London 1977

Beveridge, Erskine, *The Churchyard Memorials of Crail*, Edinburgh 1893

Brown, James, *The Epitaphs and Monumental Inscriptions in Greyfriars Churchyard, Edinburgh*, Edinburgh 1867

Burgess, Frederick, *English Churchyard Memorials*, London 1963 and SPCK 1979

Dobie, William, et al., *A Collection of Epitaphs and Monumental Inscriptions in Scotland*, Glasgow 1834

Donaldson, Islay, *East Lothian Gravestones*, East Lothian District Council 1991

Donaldson, Islay, *Midlothian Gravestones*, Midlothian District Library Service 1994

Duncan, Andrew, *Eligorium Sepulchralum Edinensium Delectus*, Edinburgh 1815

Grigson, Geoffrey, *The Faber Book of Epigrams and Epitaphs*, London 1977

Jervise, A., *Epitaphs and Inscriptions from Burial Grounds and Old Buildings in the North-East of Scotland*, Vols 1 and 2, David Douglas 1875 and 1879

Lamont-Brown, Raymond, *A New Book of Epitaphs*, 1973

Lamont-Brown, Raymond, *Scottish Epitaphs*, Chambers, Edinburgh 1990

Lindley, K.A., *Of Graves and Epitaphs*, Hutchinson 1965

Mitchell, Alison (ed.) *Monumental Inscriptions on Scottish Gravestones*, 1960 - (ongoing)

Macdonald, Sir George, 'Post Reformation Tombstones in St Andrews Cathedral Churchyard', Proc. Soc. Antiq. Scot., ixx, 1935

Monteith, Robert, *An Theater of Mortality*, Edinburgh 1704 and 1713

Pettigrew, T., The *Chronicles of the Tombs*, Vols 1 and 2, H.G. Bohn 1857

Quarles, Francis, *Emblems Divine and Moral together with Hieroglyphics of the Life of Man*, London, edn 1777

Reder, Philip, *Epitaphs*, 1969

Rees, Nigel, *A Dictionary of Grave Epigrams and Memorial Eloquence*, London 1983

Rogers, Charles, *Monuments and Monumental Inscriptions*, Griffen 1872

Sievewright, William, *Greyfriars Burial Ground, Perth: its Epitaphs and Inscriptions*, Perth 1894

Weever, J., *A Discourse of Funerall Monuments*, London 1631

Willsher, Betty and Hunter, Doreen, *Stones: 18th Century Scottish Gravestones*, Edinburgh, 1978

Willsher, Betty, *Understanding Scottish Graveyards*, Council for Scottish Archaeology, Edinburgh 1988